New York
Yankees
Baseball

By The Numbers

New York Yankees Baseball

By The Numbers

Researched by Tom P. Rippey III

Tom P. Rippey III & Paul F. Wilson, Editors

Kick The Ball, Ltd

Lewis Center, Ohio

By The Numbers Books by Kick The Ball, Ltd

College Football
Ohio State Buckeyes

Pro Baseball

Boston Red Sox	New York Yankees

Visit us online at www.ByTheNumberBook.com

This book is dedicated to our families and friends for your unwavering love, support, and your understanding of our pursuit of our passions. Thank you for everything you do for us and for making our lives complete.

New York Yankees Baseball: By The Numbers;
First Edition 2011

Published by
Kick The Ball, Ltd
8595 Columbus Pike, Suite 197
Lewis Center, OH 43035
www.ByTheNumberBook.com

Edited by: Tom P. Rippey III & Paul F. Wilson
Copy Edited by: Ashley Thomas Memory
Designed and Formatted by: Paul F. Wilson
Researched by: Tom P. Rippey III

For information on ordering this book in bulk at reduced prices, please email us at pfwilson@bythenumberbook.com.

International Standard Book Number: 978-1-934372-93-7

Printed and Bound in the United States of America

10 9 8 7 6 5 4 3 2 1

Table of Contents

About Kick The Ball, Ltd *By The Numbers* Books

"By The Numbers" books, articles, magazine features, etc. come in many formats. Most are done in pure chronological order, some match numbers in logical strings or related natural progressions within a category, and still others follow no easily discernable pattern at all.

As you turn the pages of this book, you will notice that we have categorized the numbers based on either the **final or final two digits** of each number. For example, you would find the year 1901 on page 1. The year 1910 would therefore be found on page 10, and so on.

In researching and compiling this book we found that to maintain our desired structure of a 1-100 grouping, this methodology would be necessary. Categorizing numbers 1-100 allows the reader to more quickly reference any given number based on the last digit or two, and gives us the ability to organize the data in exactly 100 pages.

This book is not meant to be exhaustive. Each researcher is given latitude to include a limited number of items they feel are particular important or interesting for each number. Additionally, other supportive or background numbers may be included with the primary number being presented. We do this to add depth to the information you are presented.

You will also notice **Featured Figure** sections spread throughout the pages of this book. These special sections include random, but interesting, information on a number relating to a particular moment or performance in team history.

All information in this book is valid
as of the end of the
2010 season.

New York Yankees

B A S E B A L L

The first game in Yankee history was against the Washington Senators on April 22, 1903. New York lost the game 1-3 and finished the season in fourth place with a 72-62 record, the team's first winning season.

The first win in Yankee history was a 7-2 victory against the Washington Senators on April 23, 1903.

The first home run in franchise history was an inside the park home run hit by John Ganzel on May 11, 1903.

New York's record against the Red Sox in 1906 was 17-5, the team's first winning season against Boston.

Derek Jeter was named MVP of the 2000 All-Star game, the first Yankee to ever win the award. Jeter went 3-for-3 while helping guide the American League to a 6-3 victory.

Johnny Damon had the first Yankee hit in the new Yankee Stadium, a line-drive single to center field in the first inning off Cleveland Indians pitcher Cliff Lee.

Derek Jeter has 101 career runs in the postseason, a Major League Baseball record. Second on the all-time MLB list is Bernie Williams, with 83 career postseason runs.

Thurman Munson hit the first home run in the remodeled old Yankee Stadium against the Twins on April 17, 1976.

By The Numbers

New York Yankees

2

B
A
S
E
B
A
L
L

New York played two seasons at Shea Stadium (1974-75) during renovations to the old Yankee Stadium. The Yankees earned a record of 90-69 for a .566 winning percentage at Shea Stadium.

Allie Reynolds threw two no-hitters in 1951, the first against the Cleveland Indians on July 12 and the second against the Boston Red Sox on Sept. 28. He is one of only four Major League pitchers to throw two no-hitters in the same season.

Only two Yankee pitchers have allowed more than 1,000 career earned runs. Red Ruffing holds the career record with 1,222 earned runs allowed and Andy Pettitte is second with 1,122 allowed.

Mickey Rivers grounded into double play two times in 1977, tying the team record set by Mickey Mantle in 1961 for the fewest times grounding into double play.

Tony Lazzeri hit two grand slams against the Philadelphia Athletics on May 24, 1932, a team single-game record.

As a team, the Yankees have hit two grand slams in a game three times, most recently against the Toronto Blue Jays on Sept. 14, 1999. The Yankees trailed 1-6 when Bernie Williams hit one in the eighth inning. Paul O'Neill hit the second one in the ninth to give New York a 10-6 win.

By The Numbers

•••ооо

New York Yankees

B A S E B A L L

Three Yankee pitchers have thrown a perfect game: Don Larsen in Game 6 of the 1956 World Series against the Brooklyn Dodgers; David Wells against the Minnesota Twins on May 17, 1998; and David Cone against the Montreal Expos on July 18, 1999.

Three Yankees have won the American League MVP Award three times: Joe DiMaggio (1939, 1941 and 1947), Yogi Berra (1951, 1954 and 1955) and Mickey Mantle (1956, 1957 and 1962).

In their first three World Series appearances, the Yankees faced the New York Giants. The Giants won the first two Series and the Yankees won the third.

The only position not represented by a Yankee in the Baseball Hall of Fame is third base.

Derek Jeter became team captain in 2003 and has continued in that position for eight consecutive years. The honorary position was previously filled by Don Mattingly from 1991-95.

The Yankees recorded 2,703 total bases in 1936 and 2009, a team record for total bases in a season.

Joe DiMaggio hit three triples against the Cleveland Indians on Aug. 27, 1938. The only other Yankees to hit three triples in a game are Hal Chase (1906) and Earle Combs (1927).

By The Numbers

• • • ○ ○ ○

New York Yankees

B
A
S
E
B
A
L
L

Lou Gehrig hit four home runs against the Philadelphia Athletics on June 3, 1932. Gehrig had six at-bats, four hits and six RBIs. Gehrig was the first American League player to accomplish this feat. Only three other AL players and eight National League players have hit four home runs in a nine inning game.

The Yankees have scored 1,000 or more runs in a season four times: 1,062 runs in 1930; 1,067 runs in 1931; 1,002 runs in 1932; and 1,065 runs in 1936.

New York has hosted the All-Star Game four times: 1939, 1960, 1977 and 2008. The AL is 1-3 at Yankee Stadium, with its only win in 1939.

Lefty Gomez led the team in strikeouts, wins, innings pitched and ERA four times (1931, 1933, 1934 and 1937). Only three other Yankees accomplished this feat more than once: Jack Chesbro (1904, 1908), Russ Ford (1910, 1911), and Spud Chandler (1943, 1946).

The Yankees have had a team batting average of .300 or higher four times: .300 in 1921; .307 in 1927; .309 in 1930; and .300 in 1936.

Mariano Rivera has only had four career plate appearances during the regular season, and has yet to record a hit as a Yankee.

By The Numbers

New York Yankees

○○○ ● ● ●

**B
A
S
E
B
A
L
L**

Five Yankee pitchers have won a Cy Young Award: Bob Turley (1958), Whitey Ford (1961), Sparky Lyle (1977), Ron Guidry (1978) and Roger Clemens (2001).

The Yankees have had nine players selected as All-Stars on five different occasions (1939, 1942, 1947, 1958 and 1959).

Babe Ruth pitched a total of five games for the Yankees, going a perfect 5-0. He only gave up one home run in 31 innings pitched as a Yankee. Ruth had a record of 89-46 as a pitcher for the Red Sox from 1914-19. He pitched 1,221.1 innings in his career and only allowed 10 home runs, just one for every 122.1 innings pitched. In comparison, Andy Pettitte has given up one home run for every 12 innings pitched during his Yankee career.

Ron Guidry is the only pitcher to have led the Yankees in strikeouts for five consecutive seasons. He led the team in strikeouts from 1977-81.

Red Ruffing hit five home runs in 1936. This is the most home runs in a season by a Yankee pitcher.

New York finished 62-15 at home in 1932 for a .805 winning percentage. This is the MLB record for highest home winning percentage in a season.

By The Numbers

● ● ● ○○○

B
A
S
E
B
A
L
L

All-time, Yankee pitchers have led the American League in saves a combined six times. Mariano Rivera led the league in saves in 1999 (45), 2001 (50) and 2004 (53). Saves became an official statistic in 1969, and the only other Yankees to lead the league in saves were Rich Gossage in 1978 (27) and 1980 (33) and Dave Righetti in 1986 (46).

New York has lost a postseason divisional series six times. The Yankees lost to the Mariners in 1995 (2-3), Indians in 1997 (2-3) and 2007 (1-3), Angels in 2002 (1-3) and 2005 (2-3) and the Tigers in 2006 (1-3).

Red Ruffing allowed 1,406 runs during his career with the Yankees, a team career record for most allowed.

Six players have played in 2,000 or more career games as a Yankee: Mickey Mantle (2,401), Derek Jeter (2,295), Lou Gehrig (2,164), Yogi Berra (2,116), Babe Ruth (2,084) and Bernie Williams (2,076).

Babe Ruth served as Yankee team captain for six days during May 20-25, 1922.

New York recorded six 1-0 wins in 1908 and 1968, a team record for most 1-0 wins in a season.

Myril Hoag hit six singles against the Red Sox on June 6, 1934, a team record for most singles hit in a game.

By The Numbers

••• ○○○

New York Yankees

B
A
S
E
B
A
L
L

The Scranton/Wilkes-Barre Yankees have been New York's AAA affiliate since 2007.

Babe Ruth led the league in runs scored seven times: 158 runs in 1920; 177 runs in 1921; 151 runs in 1923; 143 runs in 1924; 139 runs in 1926; 158 runs in 1927; and 163 runs in 1928.

New York gave up seven home runs against the Red Sox on July 4, 2003, a single-game team record for home runs allowed.

New York only played 107 regular-season games in the strike-shortened season of 1981. This is a team record for fewest games played in the regular season.

Alex Rodriguez had seven RBIs in the sixth inning against the Tampa Bay Rays on Oct. 4, 2009. This is an American League record for most RBIs in an inning.

Bill Zuber lost seven shutout games in 1945, a team record for most shutouts lost in a season.

Opposing pitching staffs have combined to throw seven no-hitters against the Yankees, most recently on June 11, 2003, when six Houston Astro pitchers combined for a no-hitter against NY. Six of the seven occurred at Yankee Stadium.

By The Numbers

● ● ● ○ ○ ○

New York Yankees

B A S E B A L L

The distance to the center field wall at Yankee Stadium is 408 feet, the same distance as the old Yankee Stadium.

New York has swept World Series opponents eight times: the Pittsburgh Pirates in 1927, St. Louis Cardinals in 1928, Chicago Cubs in 1932 and 1938, Cincinnati Reds in 1939, Philadelphia Phillies in 1950, San Diego Padres in 1998 and Atlanta Braves in 1999.

In addition to perfect games, Yankee pitchers have thrown a combined eight no-hitters: George Mogridge in 1917, Sam Jones in 1923, Monte Pearson in 1928, Allie Reynolds twice in 1951, Dave Righetti in 1983, Jim Abbott in 1993 and Dwight Gooden in 1996.

The last regular season game at the old Yankee Stadium took place on Sept. 21, 2008, against the Baltimore Orioles. New York won the game 7-3. Jose Molina hit a home run in the fourth inning, the last Yankee home run in the storied stadium. Jason Giambi recorded the last Yankee hit in the seventh inning.

Bill Dickey caught 1,708 games for the Yankees, a team record. He is followed by: Yogi Berra (1,695), Jorge Posada (1,573), Thurman Munson (1,278) and Elston Howard (1,030).

New York used eight pitchers in 1922 and 1923, a team record for fewest pitchers used in a single season.

By The Numbers

• • • ○○○

New York Yankees

**B
A
S
E
B
A
L
L**

The Yankees won their most recent World Series by beating the Phillies 4-2 in the 2009 Series.

The American League batting title has been won nine times by a Yankee: Babe Ruth (1924), Lou Gehrig (1934), Joe DiMaggio (1939, 1940), Snuffy Stirnweiss (1945), Mickey Mantle (1956), Don Mattingly (1984), Paul O'Neill (1994) and Bernie Williams (1998).

Nine Yankee managers have won a World Series: Joe McCarthy (7), Casey Stengel (7), Joe Torre (4), Miller Huggins (3), Ralph Houk (2), and one each for Billy Martin, Bucky Harris, Bob Lemon and Joe Girardi.

Joe McCarthy led New York to 809 wins at the old Yankee Stadium, a stadium record. The rest of the top five: Joe Torre (614), Casey Stengel (604), Ralph Houk (550) and Miller Huggins (339).

Hideki Matsui had three hits for six RBIs in Game 6 of the 2009 World Series, driving in all but one of the Yankees' runs in the series clinching game. This tied the World Series record set by Bobby Richardson in 1960.

The Yankees had nine 0-1 losses in 1914, a team record for most 0-1 losses in a season.

The Yankees had a .309 team batting average in 1930, the team record for highest batting average in a season.

By The Numbers

• • • ○ ○ ○

New York Yankees

B
A
S
E
B
A
L
L

The Yankees played at the Polo Grounds for 10 years, the home field of the New York Giants baseball team, from 1913-22.

Babe Ruth was American League Home Run Champion 10 times as a Yankee (54 in 1920, 59 in 1921, 41 in 1923, 46 in 1924, 47 in 1926, 60 in 1927, 54 in 1928, 46 in 1929, 49 in 1930 and 46 in 1931). His totals also led Major League Baseball every season except 1930. That year Hack Wilson of the Chicago Cubs hit 56 home runs.

Mickey Mantle struck out 1,710 times during his career as a Yankee, the most of any player. He struck out 100 or more times in seven seasons, the most was 126 in 1959.

Red Ruffing had 12 10-win seasons as a Yankee, the most of any right-handed pitcher. He finished with less than 10 wins just three times in his Yankee career.

Yankee batters hit 110 triples in 1930, a team record for most triples hit in a season. Four players hit 10 or more triples and Earle Combs led the team with 22.

Yankee batters combined to hit 10 doubles against the Blue Jays on April 12, 1988, and against the Reds on June 5, 2003. This is a team record for most doubles hit in a single game.

By The Numbers

New York Yankees

11

B
A
S
E
B
A
L
L

The Yankees played the Dodgers 11 times in the World Series (1941, 1947, 1949, 1952, 1953, 1955, 1956, 1963, 1977, 1978 and 1981). The Yankees won eight of the matchups, losing in 1955, 1963 and 1981.

A total of 11 players served as team captain of the Yankees: Hal Chase, Roger Peckingpaugh, Babe Ruth, Everett Scott, Lou Gehrig, Thurman Munson, Graig Nettles, Willie Randolph, Ron Guidry, Don Mattingly and Derek Jeter.

In the bottom of the 11th inning in Game 7 of the 2003 American League Championship Series, Aaron Boone hit a walk-off home run off Tim Wakefield of the Boston Red Sox. It was Boone's first home run of the series. Down 2-5 entering the bottom of the eighth, the Yankees rallied to tie the game 5-5. After going three up, three down in the ninth and 10th innings, Boone was the first batter in the 11th. He hit the first pitch over the left field wall to give the Yankees their 39th American League Pennant.

Tony Lazzeri hit 11 RBIs on May 24, 1936, a single-game Yankee and AL record. He hit three home runs (two of which were grand slams), a triple and a single.

Babe Ruth's career slugging percentage is .711, the highest of any Yankee. The rest of the top five: Lou Gehrig (.632), Joe DiMaggio (.579), Alex Rodriguez (.559) and Mickey Mantle (.557).

By The Numbers

• • • ○ ○ ○

New York Yankees

B
A
S
E
B
A
L
L

Twelve Yankees have been named World Series MVP: Don Larsen (1956), Bob Turley (1958), Bobby Richardson (1960), Whitey Ford (1961), Ralph Terry (1962), Reggie Jackson (1977), Bucky Dent (1978), John Wetteland (1996), Scott Brosius (1998), Mariano Rivera (1999), Derek Jeter (2000) and Hideki Matsui (2009). The award was first given in 1955.

Yankee pitchers have won Gold Glove Awards 12 times. Bobby Shantz won four Gold Gloves (1957-60), Ron Guidry won five (1982-86) and Mike Mussina won three (2001, 2003 and 2008). The first Rawlings Gold Glove was awarded in 1957.

Twelve Yankees have been American League Home Run Champion a total of 29 times: Wally Pipp (1916, 1917), Babe Ruth (1920, 1921, 1923, 1924, 1926-31) Bob Meusel (1925), Lou Gehrig (1931, 1934, 1936), Joe DiMaggio (1937, 1948), Nick Etten (1944), Mickey Mantle (1955, 1956, 1958, 1960), Roger Maris (1961), Graig Nettles (1976), Reggie Jackson (1980), Alex Rodriguez (2005, 2007) and Mark Teixeira (2009). Gehrig and Ruth tied as league leaders in 1931 with 46 home runs each.

Pinstripes have been part of the Yankee uniform since 1915. They first appeared on the uniform in 1912. They were removed, however, for the 1913 and 1914 seasons.

By The Numbers

• • • ○ ○ ○

New York Yankees

B
A
S
E
B
A
L
L

Although the nickname Yankees was used in reference to the team as early as 1904, it didn't become the official name until 1913. From 1903-12, the team was known as the Highlanders. There are two theories behind the name of Highlanders. First, the team played at Hilltop Park, which was located at 168th St. and Broadway, one of the highest points in Manhattan. Second, it connected the name of team President Joe Gordon to a famous British army regiment, The Gordon Highlanders.

New York lost 13 straight games from May 21 to June 6 of the 1913 season, the team record for consecutive games lost.

Mickey Mantle played in 1,213 career games at the old Yankee Stadium, a stadium record. The rest of the top five players: Lou Gehrig (1,080), Yogi Berra (1,068), Bernie Williams (1,039) and Derek Jeter (1,004).

Andy Pettitte and Whitey Ford each had 13 10-win seasons with the Yankees, a team record for most career 10-win seasons. Pettitte never had a season with less than 10 wins and Ford had only three (1950, 1966 and 1967).

The Yankees have played in 13 games that lasted 16 innings or more. New York's record in those games is 6-4-2.

New York allowed 13 home runs in 1907, a team record for fewest home runs allowed in a season.

By The Numbers

• • • ○ ○ ○

New York Yankees

○ ○ ○ • • •

B
A
S
E
B
A
L
L

The longest drought between American League Pennants for the Yankees was 14 years. New York failed to win a pennant from 1982-95.

Don Mattingly won a Gold Glove Award nine times (1985-89 and 1991-94) in 14 seasons as a Yankee. His nine Gold Glove Awards are the most received by any Yankee.

Jack Warhop hit 114 batters in 1,412.2 innings pitched during his career as a Yankee pitcher from 1908-15. Warhop hit 52 more batters than Tommy Byrne, the player in second place on the career list.

The Yankees allowed 14 runs in the second inning in a game against the Cleveland Indians on April 18, 2009, a single-inning team record for runs allowed.

Whitey Ford pitched a 14-inning complete-game shutout against the Washington Senators on April 22, 1959. He allowed just seven hits and struck out 15.

The Yankees beat the Mets 6-5 in Game 2 of the 2000 World Series. It was the Yankees' 14th consecutive Series victory, a franchise record.

The Yankees were shut out 27 times in 1914, a team record for most shutouts in a single season. New York finished the season with a record of 70-84 for a .455 winning percentage.

By The Numbers

• • • ○ ○ ○

New York Yankees

○○○••• ———————————————————— (15)

B
A
S
E
B
A
L
L

Yankees have hit for the cycle 15 times: Bert Daniels (July 25, 1912), Bob Meusel (May 7, 1921; July 3, 1922; and July 26, 1928), Tony Lazzeri (June 3, 1932), Lou Gehrig (June 25, 1934 and Aug. 1, 1937), Joe DiMaggio (July 9, 1937 and May 20, 1948), Buddy Rosar (July 19, 1940), Joe Gordon (Sept. 8, 1940), Mickey Mantle (July 23, 1957), Bobby Murcer (Aug. 28, 1972), Tony Fernandez (Sept. 3, 1995) and Melky Cabrera (Aug. 2, 2009).

New York has retired 15 jersey numbers to honor 16 Yankee players and managers: Billy Martin (No. 1), Babe Ruth (No. 3), Lou Gehrig (No. 4), Joe DiMaggio (No. 5), Mickey Mantle (No. 7), Yogi Berra (No. 8), Bill Dickey (No. 8), Roger Maris (No. 9), Phil Rizzuto (No. 10), Thurman Munson (No. 15), Whitey Ford (No. 16), Don Mattingly (No. 23), Elston Howard (No. 32), Casey Stengel (No. 37), Reggie Jackson (No. 44) and Ron Guidry (No. 49). In addition, jersey No. 42 was retired by all Major League Baseball teams in 1997 to honor Jackie Robinson's 50th anniversary of becoming the first black player in MLB.

Yogi Berra was an American League All-Star selection 15 consecutive years, from 1948-62. He only played three years as a Yankee without being named an All-Star (1946, 1947 and 1963).

New York lost 15 home games in 1932, a team record for fewest home losses in a season.

By The Numbers

———————————————————— •••○○○

New York Yankees

16

B
A
S
E
B
A
L
L

Joe McCarthy had the longest tenure as manager of the Yankees. He managed the team for 16 seasons, from 1931-46.

Whitey Ford played 16 seasons for the Yankees (1950, 1953-67). He earned a career record of 236-106 for a .690 winning percentage, the winningest left-handed pitcher in the 20th Century.

The 2010 season marked the 16th consecutive season with the Yankees for Derek Jeter, Jorge Posada and Mariano Rivera.

Yankee players were walked 16 times against the Philadelphia Athletics on June 23, 1915, a team record for most bases on balls in a single game.

David Cone recorded 16 strikeouts against the Detroit Tigers on June 23, 1997, a team record for most strikeouts in a game by a right-handed pitcher.

Johnny Lindell and Snuffy Strinweiss each had 16 triples in 1944 and tied as American League leaders in this category.

Wally Pipp led Major League Baseball with 12 home runs in 1916.

Whitey Ford's No. 16 jersey was retired by the Yankees in 1974. He was elected into the Baseball Hall of Fame in the same year.

By The Numbers

• • • ○ ○ ○

New York Yankees

B A S E B A L L

The longest drought between World Series Championships for the Yankees is 17 years. New York failed to win a Series from 1979-95.

Babe Ruth and Roy White hold the Yankee record for times caught stealing in a career with 117. Only two other Yankees have been caught stealing 100 or more times in their career: Bob Meusel (102) and Lou Gehrig (101).

Spud Chandler is the winningest Yankee pitcher with at least 100 starts. He went 109-43 as a Yankee pitcher from 1937-47 for a .717 winning percentage. His career ERA was 2.84 and he allowed just 64 home runs in 1,485 innings pitched, or one in every 23.2 innings.

The Yankees had 5,717 at-bats in 2007, a team single-season record for most at-bats. The team's batting average was .290 with 968 runs scored that season.

New York lost 17 consecutive home games in 1913, a team record for most consecutive home losses in a season.

The Yankees have finished in first place and failed to win the World Series 17 times (1921, 1922, 1926, 1942, 1955, 1957, 1960, 1963, 1964, 1976, 1980 and 2001-06).

Wally Pipp led the American League with nine home runs in 1917. It was the last time any player led the AL with a single-digit home run total for the season.

By The Numbers

●●● ○ ○ ○

New York Yankees

○○○ • • • ──────────────────────── 〔18〕

B
A
S
E
B
A
L
L

Ron Guidry struck out 18 California Angel batters on June 17, 1978, a single-game Yankee record. He pitched a complete game and allowed just four hits while walking two. The 4-0 Yankee victory was Guidry's 11th win of the season. He wouldn't lose a game until July 7 and finished the season 25-3, winning the American League Cy Young Award.

Red Rolfe scored in 18 consecutive games in 1939, a single-season team record. That season, Rolfe also led the team in runs scored, hits, doubles, triples and walks.

Andy Pettitte has 18 career postseason wins as a Yankee, a team record. His record as a Yankee in the postseason is 18-9 for a .667 winning percentage.

Yankee base runners were caught stealing 18 times in 1961 and 1964, a team record for fewest times in a season. Only four players were caught stealing more than once for each of the two seasons.

Derek Jeter has 5,718 career assists, a team record. He is followed on the career list by: Willie Randolph (4,996), Tony Lazzeri (4,810), Frank Crosetti (4,696) and Phil Rizzuto (4,666).

New York changed managers 18 times from 1978-92. Billy Martin managed the team five different times and Lou Piniella, Bob Lemon and Gene Michael each managed two times.

By The Numbers

• • • ○○○

New York Yankees

○○○••• ————————————————— ⊕ 19

BASEBALL

Nineteen players have been inducted into the Baseball Hall of Fame with the Yankees as their primary team: Babe Ruth (1936), Lou Gehrig (1939), Willie Keeler (1939), Jack Chesbro (1946), Herb Pennock (1948), Bill Dickey (1954), Joe DiMaggio (1955), Red Ruffing (1967), Waite Hoyte (1969), Earle Combs (1970), Yogi Berra (1972), Whitey Ford (1972), Lefty Gomez (1972), Mickey Mantle (1974), Tony Lazzeri (1991), Phil Rizzuto (1994), Dave Winfield (2001), Rich Gossage (2008) and Joe Gordon (2009).

New York won 19 straight games from June 29 to July 17 of the 1947 season, the team record for consecutive games won.

Babe Ruth had 119 extra-base hits in 1921, a Yankee single-season record. He had 44 doubles, 16 triples and 59 home runs.

New York went 52-29 at home in 2010, the team's 19th consecutive winning season at home. The Yankees finished 39-42 at home in 1991, their last losing season at home.

New York finished the season with 19 wins on the road in 1912, a franchise record for fewest road wins in a season.

Willie Randolph reached base on balls 119 times in 1980, a team single-season record for right-handed batters.

By The Numbers

••• ○○○

New York Yankees

○ ○ ○ • • •

B A S E B A L L

New York's home attendance more than doubled in Babe Ruth's first season as a Yankee in 1920. Home attendance went from just over 619,000 in 1919 to over 1,289,000 in 1920.

Only four Yankees have recorded 20 or more doubles in a single-season. Earle Combs set the single-season team record with 23 in 1927. He also recorded 22 in 1930 and 21 in 1928. The only other players to have 20 or more are Lou Gehrig (20 in 1926), Snuffy Stirnweiss (22 in 1945) and Birdie Cree (22 in 1911).

Dioner Navarro made his major league debut with the Yankees on Sept. 7, 2004. He was 20 years and 211 days old, making him the youngest Yankee since 1985 to debut in Major League Baseball.

New York stranded 1,010 runners on base in 1920, a team record for fewest batters left on base in a season.

Yankee pitchers have won 20 or more games in a season 59 times. CC Sabathia won 21 games in 2010 and is the most recent player to accomplish this feat.

The Yankees lost just 20 road games in 1939, a team record for fewest road losses in a season. In comparison, New York lost 25 games at home that year.

By The Numbers

• • • ○ ○ ○

New York Yankees

BASEBALL

New York won its first American League pennant in 1921. The Yankees finished the season with a 98-55 record, 4 ½ games ahead of the Cleveland Indians. In the World Series, the Yankees beat the New York Giants by the score of 3-0 in both Game 1 and Game 2. The Giants won the next two games before the Yankees took the Series advantage in Game 5. However, the Giants won the next three games, two by just one run, to win the best of nine series.

From an early age, Lou Gehrig showed athletic ability in both baseball and football. In 1921 he left home to attend Columbia University on a football scholarship. Before the first semester even began he was swayed by the manager of the New York Giants to play minor league baseball with the Hartford Senators. Risking his football scholarship, Gehrig changed his name to Henry Lewis, but was later discovered and banned from intercollegiate play his freshman year. The following year he was allowed to suit up as a fullback for the Columbia Lions. However, it was not too long before Gehrig's true calling rose above all other competing interests. In his sophomore year, he began playing baseball for Columbia and earned a .444 batting average. Gehrig also struck out 17 batters in a game he pitched for the Lions, a single-game record at Columbia to this day. Soon after he was signed by the Yankees and history was made.

By The Numbers

•••ooo

New York Yankees

B A S E B A L L

Yankee players have been named American League Most Valuable Player 22 times: Babe Ruth (1923), Lou Gehrig (1927, 1936), Joe DiMaggio (1939, 1941, 1947), Joe Gordon (1942), Spud Chandler (1943), Phil Rizzuto (1950), Yogi Berra (1951, 1954, 1955), Mickey Mantle (1956, 1957, 1962), Roger Maris (1960, 1961), Elston Howard (1963), Thurman Munson (1976), Don Mattingly (1985) and Alex Rodriguez (2005, 2007).

The Yankees and Detroit Tigers played a 22-inning game on June 24, 1962, the longest game by innings in New York history. The game was tied 7-7 at the end of nine innings. New York's Jim Bouton entered the game in the 16th inning and finished the game. He faced 26 batters, walked two, struck out six, and allowed just three hits. Jack Reed hit a two-run home run in the top of the 22nd inning to give the Yankees the lead. Bouton received the win after Johnny Blanchard recorded the last out, a fly ball hit by Norm Cash. The game lasted a team record 7 hours.

The New York Yankees and New York Giants played a tie game in Game 2 of the 1922 World Series. Yankee pitcher Jesse Barnes allowed a three-run home run in the first inning, followed by nine scoreless innings. However, with the score tied 3-3 after 10 innings, the umpire called the game due to darkness. The Giants went on the win the Series 4-0.

By The Numbers

•••○○○

New York Yankees

23

B A S E B A L L

Old Yankee Stadium officially opened on April 18, 1923, and 74,200 fans went through the turnstiles to watch the Yankees beat the Red Sox 4-1. The Yankees' Bob Shawkey pitched a complete game and was the winning pitcher, striking out five and walking two. Babe Ruth hit the first, and only, home run of the day, pushing New York's lead to 4-0 in the bottom of the third.

The Yankees won their first World Series title in 1923 after beating the New York Giants 4-2. This was the third consecutive season that the two teams had met in the World Series. Although the Giants won the third game to take a 2-1 series lead, the Yankees outscored the Giants 22-9 in the next three games to win the franchise's first Series title. As a team, the Yankees had a .293 batting average and limited the Giants to a .234 batting average.

Lou Gehrig hit 23 grand slams in his career as a Yankee, a franchise record.

New York has played the Detroit Tigers 1,923 times in the regular season. The Yankees lead the series 1,020-914 for a .530 winning percentage, the lowest among American League opponents played 500 times or more.

Mariano Rivera has a 2.23 career ERA, a team record. The rest of the top five: Russ Ford (2.54), Jack Chesbro (2.58), Al Orth and Ernie Bonham (both 2.72) and George Mogridge (2.73).

By The Numbers

•••ooo

New York Yankees

B A S E B A L L

The Yankees lost 6-24 against the Cleveland Indians on July 29, 1928, the most runs ever allowed by New York in a single game. The Indians led 17-1 after two innings and had 27 hits in 8 ½ innings.

Derek Jeter hit 24 home runs in 1999, his single-season career high and the most hit in a single season by a Yankee shortstop. Jeter has hit 20 or more home runs in a season just two other times in his career: 21 in 2001 and 23 in 2004.

New York lost 24 games in July 1908, a team record for most losses in a single month. The team finished the season with a record of 51-103 for a .331 winning percentage.

The Yankees shut out the opposing team 24 times in 1951, a team record for most shutouts in a season.

Yankee base runners stole base 24 times in 1948, a team record for fewest in a season. Phil Rizzuto led the team with five stolen bases, and only six players stole more than one base.

Yankee batters struck out 420 times in 1924, a team record for fewest strikeouts in a season. Babe Ruth was the only batter with more than 50 strikeouts for the season. He led the team with 81.

By The Numbers

New York Yankees

○ ○ ○ • • • ————————————

B
A
S
E
B
A
L
L

The Yankees scored 25 runs against the Philadelphia Athletics on May 24, 1936, a team record for runs scored in a nine-inning game.

Five Yankees hit 25 or more home runs in 2009: Mark Teixeira (39), Alex Rodriguez (30), Nick Swisher (29), Hideki Matsui (28) and Robinson Cano (25). This is a team single-season record for most players with 25 or more home runs. The previous record was in 1938 when Bill Dickey (27), Joe DiMaggio (32), Lou Gehrig (29) and Joe Gordon (25) hit the mark.

The longest 1-0 game won by the Yankees took place on July 4, 1925. New York beat the Philadelphia Athletics 1-0 in 15 innings.

The Yankees used 25 players throughout the season in 1923 and 1927, a team record for fewest players used in a single season.

The Yankees hit a home run in 25 consecutive games in 1940, a team record for home runs in consecutive games. The team hit a total of 40 home runs during the streak.

In 1995 Paul O'Neill led Major League Baseball in times grounded into double play with 25. It is the only time a Yankee has led the league in this category.

By The Numbers

————————————— • • • ○ ○ ○

rk Yankees

S
E
B
A
L
L

...erson holds the Yankee record ...olen bases. Henderson played with ...ankees from 1985-89 and stole 326 bases. The rest of the top five in career stolen bases: Derek Jeter (232), Willie Randolph (251), Hal Chase (248) and Roy White (233). The closest active player on the 2010 roster following Jeter was Alex Rodriguez with 124 career stolen bases as a Yankee.

Wally Pipp recorded 226 career sacrifice hits, a Yankee record. The most he hit in a single-season was 33 in 1921.

Red Ruffing recorded 126 career wins at the old Yankee Stadium, a stadium record. The rest of the top five: Whitey Ford (120), Lefty Gomez (112), Ron Guidry (99) and Andy Pettitte (94).

Jack Warhop hit 26 batters in 1909, a team single-season record. The other starting pitchers that season combined for 26 batters hit.

Derek Jeter has 2,926 career hits as a Yankee, a team record. He recorded 219 hits in 1999, his career single-season high and a team record for most hits in a season by a right-handed batter. The only other players with 2,000 or more hits: Lou Gehrig (2,721) Babe Ruth (2,518), Mickey Mantle (2,415), Bernie Williams (2,336), Joe DiMaggio (2,214), Don Mattingly (2,153) and Yogi Berra (2,148).

By The Numbers

• • • ○ ○ ○

New York Yankees

BASEBALL

New York won its 27th World Series in 2009 after beating the Philadelphia Phillies 4-2. The other franchises in the top four in Major League Baseball with the most titles (Cardinals, Athletics and Red Sox) combine for just 26 World Series titles. Yankees World Series titles: 1923, 1927, 1928, 1932, 1936, 1937, 1938, 1939, 1941, 1943, 1947, 1949, 1950, 1951, 1952, 1953, 1956, 1958, 1961, 1962, 1977, 1978, 1996, 1998, 1999, 2000 and 2009.

Sam Jones allowed 127 earned runs in 1925, a team single-season record for most allowed. Jones also led the starting rotation in highest ERA (4.63), most runs scored (147), most batters walked (104) and most strikeouts (92).

In 1913 New York finished with 27 wins at home, a franchise record for fewest home wins in a season. They finished with a 27-47 home record for a .365 winning percentage.

New York recorded 327 doubles as a team in 2006, the team record for most doubles in a season. Eight players hit 25 or more doubles for the season. Robinson Cano led the team with 41 doubles.

The Yankees pitching staff allowed 27 hits against the Red Sox on May 28, 2005, a team record for most hits allowed in a home game. Carl Pavano started for the Yankees and allowed 11 hits in 3.2 innings.

By The Numbers

●●●○○○

New York Yankees

B
A
S
E
B
A
L
L

The Notre Dame Fighting Irish and Army Cadet football teams played at Yankee Stadium on Nov. 12, 1928. Army entered the game undefeated, riding an 11-game winning streak. Notre Dame was 4-2 and the school had not lost more than two games in a season for 22 seasons. Entering halftime tied 0-0, Knute Rockne gave the famous "Win One for the Gipper" speech. Notre Dame rallied in the second half, defeating Army 12-6. The two teams met 22 times in the old Yankee Stadium with Notre Dame holding a 14-5-3 advantage.

Whitey Ford allowed 228 home runs during his New York career. He allowed 15 or fewer home runs in 11 of his 16 seasons. Only three other Yankees have allowed 200 or more career home runs: Red Ruffing (200), Andy Pettitte (211) and Ron Guidry (226).

New York won 28 games in August 1938, a team record for most wins in a month during the season.

New York used 28 pitchers throughout the season in 2005 and 2007, a team record for most pitchers used in a single season.

The Yankees allowed 28 hits to the Detroit Tigers on Sept. 29, 1928, a team single-game record.

Alex Rodriguez hit 28 home runs on the road in 2007, a team single-season record for right-handed batters.

By The Numbers

• • • ○ ○ ○

New York Yankees

B
A
S
E
B
A
L
L

Yankee pitchers have recorded 29 hits in 276 at-bats in interleague play for a combined batting average of .095.

The Yankees first added numbers to their jerseys in 1929. Initial distribution of numbers was based on a player's position in the batting order. So in 1929, Earle Combs received No. 1, Mark Koenig No. 2, Babe Ruth No. 3, Lou Gehrig No. 4, Bob Meusel No. 5, Tony Lazzeri No. 6, Leo Durocher No. 7, Johnny Grabowski No. 8, Benny Bengough No. 9 and Bill Dickey No. 10.

Joe DiMaggio hit 29 home runs in 1936, a team record for most home runs in a season by a rookie. He surpassed that season total in each of his next five seasons.

Lou Gehrig hit 126 RBIs in 1929, the only season he did not lead Major League Baseball in this category from 1927-31.

Thurman Munson had 229 doubles in 11 seasons with the Yankees, 15 or more in each of his last 10 seasons.

Featured Figure

The largest deficit overcome in a Yankee victory is nine runs. This has happened three times, most recently against the Texas Rangers on May 16, 2006, when the Yankees trailed 0-9 in the bottom of the second inning and won the game 14-13. A three-run home run hit by Derek Jeter in the sixth inning sparked a six-run rally in the inning.

By The Numbers

• • • ○ ○ ○

New York Yankees

B A S E B A L L

Lou Gehrig's Major League Baseball record of 2,130 consecutive games played would stand for 56 years until broken by Cal Ripken, Jr. on Sept. 6, 1995. Gehrig's streak began when he replaced first baseman Wally Pipp in the lineup on June 1, 1925. The last game in his streak was against the Senators on April 30, 1939. The "Iron Horse" removed himself from the lineup on May 2, 1939. He was replaced at first base by Babe Dahlgren who played 327 games with the Yankees from 1937-40.

Roger Maris hit 30 home runs at the old Yankee Stadium in 1961, tying the single-season record set by Lou Gehrig in 1930 for most home runs by a Yankee in the stadium.

Mariano Rivera had 230 saves at the old Yankee Stadium, a stadium record since saves became an official stat in 1969. The rest of the top five: Dave Righetti (111), Goose Gossage (70), Sparky Lyle (63) and Steve Farr (45).

The Yankees allowed 1,566 hits in 1930, a team single-season record for most hits allowed. Six pitchers allowed more than 175 hits for the season.

Dave Winfield grounded into double play 30 times in 1983, the team single-season record.

Mickey Mantle hit 30 home runs on the road in 1961, a team single-season record for switch-hitter batters.

By The Numbers

New York Yankees

**B
A
S
E
B
A
L
L**

Joe DiMaggio played for the Yankees from 1936-42 and 1946-51. The team failed to make the World Series just three times during DiMaggio's days as a Yankee (1940, 1946 and 1948). DiMaggio was unable to play for the Yankees from 1943-45 after joining the Army to serve in World War II, where he served 31 months and rose to the rank of Sergeant.

Ben Chapman holds the Yankee record for most times hit by pitch in a season. Chapman was hit by pitch 23 times in 1931.

Babe Ruth holds the Yankee career record for total bases. He touched 5,131 total bases in his career with New York.

Clark Griffith was the first manager of the Yankees. He managed New York from 1903-08 with a combined record of 419-370 for a .531 winning percentage. Griffith also pitched 483 innings for the Yankees from 1903-07. During that time, he pitched 35 complete games of 44 games started and had an ERA of 2.66.

Earl Combs led the American League with 231 hits in 1927. He was the first Yankee to lead the league in hits. Only seven other Yankees have accomplished this feat: Lou Gehrig (1931), Red Rolfe (1939), Snuffy Stirnweiss (1944 and 1945), Bobby Richardson (1962), Don Mattingly (1984 and 1986), Derek Jeter (1999) and Alfonso Soriano (2002).

By The Numbers

•••○○○

New York Yankees

B
A
S
E
B
A
L
L

A granite monument was dedicated at Yankee Stadium in 1932 to honor former Yankee manager Miller Huggins. This was the beginning of what would become Monument Park. Gehrig and Ruth were honored with monuments in 1941 and 1949 respectively. These three monuments were placed on the playing field, just inside the center field wall. Following renovations in 1976, the monuments, along with plaques dedicated to other players and those who have faithfully served the franchise over the years, were moved to an area behind the center field wall. It wasn't until 1985 that fans could walk through this area. Four other monuments have since been added: Mickey Mantle (1996), Joe DiMaggio (1999), one in remembrance of Sept. 11, 2001 (2002), and one in honor of George Steinbrenner (2010). All monuments and plaques were moved to the new stadium behind the center field wall, where they may be viewed by the public before, during and after home games.

Red Ruffing pitched a 10-inning shutout and hit a home run to give the Yankees a 1-0 win against the Washington Senators on Aug. 13, 1932. He is the last pitcher in Major League Baseball to pitch a complete game shutout and hit a home run in the same game.

Babe Ruth and Lou Gehrig each hit two home runs in Game 3 of the 1932 World Series against the Chicago Cubs. Ruth gestured to the bleachers before hitting his second home run, now known as the "called shot."

By The Numbers

New York Yankees

B A S E B A L L

New York has played teams currently in the National League a total of 633 times in the regular season. The Yankees are 351-282 against NL teams for a .555 winning percentage.

New York has played the Milwaukee Brewers 390 times, the most games against any current NL team. The Brewers were part of the American League before moving to the NL following Major League Baseball expansion in 1998. The Yankees are 208-182 all-time against the Brewers for a .533 winning percentage.

The Yankees lost 0-7 to the Philadelphia Athletics on Aug. 3, 1933. This ended a 308-game streak without being shut out that started exactly two years earlier.

The Yankees turned a triple play on April 22, 2010, against the Oakland A's. It was their first triple play in 6,633 games. New York's previous triple play took place on June 3, 1968.

Casey Stengel went 10-2 on opening day for a .833 winning percentage, the highest among managers with 10 or more opening games with the Yankees.

Ben Chapman led MLB with 27 steals in 1933. It was his third consecutive season leading the league in this category. He had 61 steals in 1931 and 38 in 1932. Chapman also led the league in times caught stealing each of these three seasons.

By The Numbers

•••○○○

33

New York Yankees

B
A
S
E
B
A
L
L

Lefty Gomez is the only Yankee pitcher to have won the American League Triple Crown. He won the award in 1934 (2.33 ERA, 26 wins, and 158 strikeouts) and again in 1937 (2.33 ERA, 21 wins, and 194 strikeouts).

Lou Gehrig hit a Yankee record 534 doubles during his career. The most he hit in a single-season was 52. The rest of the top five on the career doubles list: Derek Jeter (468), Bernie Williams (449), Don Mattingly (442) and Babe Ruth (424).

Lou Gehrig won the AL Triple Crown in 1934. He had 210 hits on 579 at-bats for a .363 batting average. He scored 128 runs and recorded 165 RBIs. Gehirg had 40 doubles, six triples and led Major League Baseball with 49 home runs.

Johnny Damon went 6-for-6 on June 7, 2008. He is the only Yankee to have recorded six hits is at the old Yankee Stadium.

New York acquired Joe DiMaggio from the San Francisco Seals on Nov. 21, 1934, for $50,000. Fifteen years later DiMaggio became the first baseball player to sign a contract for $100,000. He signed a one-year, $100,000 contract for each of his last three seasons.

By The Numbers

● ● ● ○ ○ ○

New York Yankees

B
A
S
E
B
A
L
L

Babe Ruth was traded to the Boston Braves in 1935 where he played one last season before retiring. He played in 28 games for the Braves, hitting six home runs and batting .181.

Derek Jeter has grounded into double play 235 times in his career, a New York record. Jeter grounded into double play 24 times in 2008, his career single-season high. The rest of the top five career list for grounded into double play: Bernie Williams (223), Don Mattingly (191), Paul O'Neill (175) and Willie Randolph (171).

The Baltimore Orioles franchise folded following the 1902 season. Bill Devery and Frank Ferrell bought the franchise and moved it to New York. In its two seasons, the folded franchise had a record of 118-153 for a .435 winning percentage.

The Yankees had 5,551 total chances in 1935, a team record for fewest in a season. Only three players had more than 500 chances for the season.

Sparky Lyle led the American League with 35 saves in 1972, the first Yankee to lead the AL in this category.

Red Ruffing had 37 hits on 109 at-bats for a .339 batting average in 1935, a team record for highest batting average in a season by a pitcher.

By The Numbers

• • • ○ ○ ○

New York Yankees

B A S E B A L L

Derek Jeter hit his first and only grand slam for the Yankees off Chicago Cubs pitcher Joe Borowski in the sixth inning on June 18, 2005. This was Jeter's 136th career at-bat with the bases loaded.

Joe DiMaggio wore jersey No. 9 in 1936, his first season with New York. He switched to No. 5 and wore that number throughout the remainder of his career. The Yankees retired his number in 1952. DiMaggio spent his entire career with the Yankees and was a two-time batting champion and three-time MVP. He was elected to the Baseball Hall of Fame in 1955.

Don Mattingly was intentionally walked 136 times in his career, a Yankee record. The most times he was intentionally walked in a single season was 18 in 1989. This stat was first recorded in 1955.

Whitey Ford had 236 career wins as a Yankee, the most of any player. Ford only had two seasons with more than 19 wins, 25 in 1961 and 24 in 1963.

The Yankees recorded 1,136 hits as a team in 1903, a team record for fewest hits in a season. The team had 4,565 at-bats for a .249 batting average.

New York had an overall record of 970-554 in the 1930s for a .636 winning percentage, representing the decade the Yankees had the best winning percentage.

By The Numbers

● ● ● ○ ○ ○

New York Yankees

○○○ ●●●

B
A
S
E
B
A
L
L

Joe DiMaggio was first referred to as the "Yankee Clipper" in 1937 by radio broadcaster Arch McDonald.

The Yankees hit 1,237 singles as a team in 1988, a franchise record for most singles hit in a season. The team recorded 1,469 total hits, of which 84.2 percent were singles.

Opposing batters recorded 337 hits against Jack Chesbro in 1904, a Yankee record for most hits against a pitcher in a single season.

Mickey Mantle led the American League with 37 home runs in 1955. It was the first of four seasons that he would lead the AL in this category. Only Babe Ruth has led the AL in home runs more seasons than Mantle.

The Yankees beat the New York Giants 4-1 in the 1937 World Series, outscoring the Giants 21-3 in the first three games. Lou Gehrig, Lefty Gomez, Myril Hoag and Joe DiMaggio all hit single-run home runs in Game 5. Mel Ott of the Giants hit a two-run home run in the third, his team's only runs. The Yankees won the game 4-2.

Featured Figure

New York won 15 consecutive road games in 1953, a team record for most consecutive road wins in a season.

By The Numbers

●●● ○○○

37

New York Yankees

B
A
S
E
B
A
L
L

Whitey Ford started in 438 games as a Yankee pitcher, a team record. He started in 28 or more games in 12 of his 16 seasons.

Don Mattingly had 238 hits in 1986, a Yankee single-season record. He also led the team in RBIs (113) and batting average (.352). His hit total also led the American League. He is the only Yankee to have led the AL in hits during two different seasons. Mattingly led the AL with 207 hits in 1984.

Monte Pearson pitched the first no-hitter by a Yankee at Yankee Stadium on Aug. 27, 1938.

Andy Pettitte has pitched in 38 career postseason games as a Yankee, a team career record. He allowed 244 hits in 237.9 postseason innings pitched.

Red Ruffing led the AL with 21 wins in 1938.

New York swept the Chicago Cubs in the 1938 World Series. The Yankees outscored the Cubs 22-9 and the Yankee pitching staff had a 1.75 ERA over the Series.

Featured Figure

Both Reggie Jackson and Babe Ruth have each hit three home runs in a World Series game, a Yankee record. Jackson hit three in Game 6 of the 1977 World Series and Ruth hit three in Game 4 of both the 1926 and 1928 World Series.

By The Numbers

New York Yankees

ooo•••

(39)

B
A
S
E
B
A
L
L

The Yankees held "Lou Gehrig Appreciation Day" on July 4, 1939. Two weeks earlier, Gehrig was diagnosed with amyotrophic lateral sclerosis, now referred to as "Lou Gehrig's Disease." However, the incurable, debilitating disease was defeated for a brief moment when, before more than 60,000 fans at Yankee Stadium that special day, he uttered the words, "Today I consider myself the luckiest man on the face of the earth." The Baseball Writers Association waived the required five-year waiting period and elected Gehrig to the Baseball Hall of Fame on Dec. 8, 1939. Gehrig is the only Yankee to have worn jersey No. 4, and it was retired by New York in 1939. Gehrig played for the Yankees from 1929-39.

Mel Stottlemyer holds the Yankee record for career losses with 139. In 11 seasons, he had less than 12 losses just three times: 1964 (3), 1965 (9) and 1974 (7).

Alfonso Soriano hit 39 home runs in 2002, a team single-season record for home runs hit by a second baseman.

New York has played the Baltimore Orioles 2,039 times in the regular season, the most games played for New York against any team in Major League Baseball. The Yankees lead the series 1,221-818 for a .599 winning percentage, the highest among American League opponents played 500 times or more.

By The Numbers

•••ooo

New York Yankees

40

B
A
S
E
B
A
L
L

The Yankees have won 40 American League pennants, more than the next three franchises combined.

The lowest regular-season winning percentage of a World Series winning Yankee team was .540. New York finished the 2000 season with a record of 87-74. After defeating the Oakland Athletics in the AL Division Series and the Seattle Mariners in the AL Championship Series, the Yankees beat the New York Mets 4-1 in the World Series.

Yogi Berra managed the Yankees in 340 regular-season games from 1964, 1984-85. He led the team to a record of 192-148 for a .565 winning percentage. New York won the 1964 AL Pennant under Berra but lost to the Cardinals in the World Series.

The Yankee pitching staff recorded 40 consecutive shutout innings in 1932, a team record. The team pitched 11 shutout games that season.

Joe DiMaggio was AL Batting Champion in 1940. He had 179 hits on 508 at-bats for a .352 batting average , and he scored 93 runs and recorded 133 RBIs. DiMaggio had 28 doubles, nine triples and 31 home runs. It was his second AL Batting Champion Title and he is the only Yankee to have won the title more than once.

By The Numbers

• • • ○ ○ ○

New York Yankees

B
A
S
E
Jack Chesbro won 41 games in 1904, the Yankee record for most wins in a season. Chesbro finished with a record of 41-21. The rest of the top five: Al Orth (27), Carl Mays (27) and seasons of 26 wins by Russ Ford, Carl Mays, Joe Bush and Lefty Gomez.

B
A
L
L
Lou Gehrig succumbed to his illness on June 2, 1941, just 17 days before turning 38. Ironically, his death was 16 years to the day that he began his historic streak of consecutive games played.

Bernie Williams played in 841 games in the outfield, the most of any Yankee since 2000. He is followed by Hideki Matsui (632) and Melky Cabrera (559).

The Yankees beat the Dodgers 4-1 in the 1941 World Series. It was only the fourth time in Major League Baseball history that two teams with 100 or more wins met in the Series. Each of the first three games were decided by a single run. The Dodgers were held to a .182 batting average for the Series, far below their regular season .272 average. It was the first of 11 World Series matchups between the two franchises.

Featured Figure

Yankee managers who lasted one season or less had a combined record of 432-468, for a .480 winning percentage.

By The Numbers

• • • ○ ○ ○

New York Yankees

42

B A S E B A L L

Mariano Rivera is the last player in Major League Baseball to wear No. 42 as his official number. The number was retired by every major league team in 1997 to honor the 50th anniversary of Jackie Robinson becoming the first black player in MLB. Rivera, wearing the number since 1995, is allowed to wear the jersey number until retirement. Since 2007, other players, managers and umpires are allowed to wear No. 42 only on April 15, which is dedicated as "Jackie Robinson Day" to honor the date of his first game.

Mariano Rivera has recorded 42 career-postseason saves, a New York record.

The Yankees allowed just 507 runs in 1942, the team record for fewest runs allowed in a season. This also ranked first in the American League that season.

New York won 18 consecutive home games in 1942, a team record for most consecutive home wins in a season.

New York has played the Tampa Bay Rays 218 times, the fewest games against any team in MLB. The Yankees hold an all-time advantage of 140-78 for a .642 winning percentage.

Willie Keeler had 42 sacrifice hits in 1905, a Yankee single-season record. He hit more than 25 sacrifice hits in five of his seven seasons with the Yankees.

By The Numbers

New York Yankees

B
A
S
E
B
A
L
L

The largest single-season home attendance at the old Yankee Stadium was 4,298,543 fans in 2008.

Joe DiMaggio announced that he would enlist in the Army prior to the start of the 1943 season. Nick Etten wore No. 5 from 1943-45 but switched to No. 9 when DiMaggio returned to the team in 1946. Etten was American League Home Run Champion in 1944 with 22 home runs, and his name is sandwiched between DiMaggio's on the list of Yankee AL Home Run Champions. DiMaggio was Home Run Champion in 1937 (46) and 1948 (39), his only seasons leading the AL in home runs.

Spud Chandler was named AL Most Valuable Player as a pitcher in 1943. He is the only Yankee pitcher to have received the honor. Chandler had a record of 20-4 for a .833 winning percentage. He allowed 197 hits, 62 runs and 46 earned runs. Chandler recorded 134 strikeouts in 253 innings pitched and had a 1.64 ERA, a Yankee single-season record for lowest ERA. He also hit two home runs and had 25 hits on 97 at-bats for a .258 batting average. His ERA and total wins were also league highs that season.

New York recorded 17 walk-off wins in 1943, a single-season team record.

By The Numbers

New York Yankees

○ ○ ○ ● ● ●

B
A
S
E
B
A
L
L

The Yankees finished the 1927 season with a record of 110-44. This represents the fewest losses in a season in Yankee history.

Mark Teixeira recorded 344 total bases in 2009, the most in the American League. It was the 23rd time a Yankee has led the AL in total bases: Babe Ruth (1921, 1923, 1924, 1926 and 1928), Lour Gehrig (1927, 1930, 1931 and 1934), Joe DiMaggio (1937, 1941 and 1948), Johnny Lindell (1944), Snuffy Stirnweiss (1945), Mickey Mantle (1956, 1958 and 1960), Roger Maris (1961), Bobby Murcer (1972), Don Mattingly (1985 and 1986) and Alex Rodriguez (2007).

The Yankees hit 244 home runs in 2009, a New York record for team home runs in a season. Seven players had more than 20 home runs. Mark Teixeira led the team with 39.

New York retired No. 44 in honor of Reggie Jackson in 1993. Jackson had a postseason .328 batting average and hit 12 home runs in 34 postseason games with the Yankees, earning him the nickname "Mr. October." He was elected to the Baseball Hall of Fame in the same year.

Don Mattingly led the AL with 44 doubles in 1984, the first of three consecutive seasons that he led the league in this category.

By The Numbers

● ● ● ○ ○ ○

New York Yankees

B
A
S
E
B
A
L
L

The Yankees have finished in first place in their division 45 times, most recently in 2009.

Whitey Ford recorded 45 career shutouts as a Yankee, a team record. He recorded eight shutouts in 1964, his career single-season high.

The longest nine-inning Yankee game lasted 4 hours and 45 minutes. It took place on Aug. 18, 2006, at Boston's Fenway Park.

Don Mattingly hit 145 RBIs in 1985, the most of any Yankee throughout the 1980s.

Bob Shawkey led the American League in 1920 with a 2.45 ERA, the first Yankee to lead the AL. It has since been done 12 other times, most recently by Dave Righetti in 1981. Lefty Gomez, Whitey Ford and Ron Guidry have each led the AL twice, the most of any Yankee.

The Yankees franchise was purchased by Dan Topping, Del Webb and Larry MacPhail in 1945 for $2.8 million.

The Yankees and Detroit Tigers combined for 45 hits on Sept. 29, 1928, a team record for most combined hits in a single game. Yankee batters accounted for 17 of the 45 hits.

By The Numbers

New York Yankees

46

B
A
S
E
B
A
L
L

The first night game at Yankee Stadium took place on May 28, 1946. New York lost their first home game under the lights 1-2 to the Washington Senators.

Red Rolfe led the American League with 46 doubles in 1939. He is the only Yankee other than Lou Gehrig and Don Mattingly to lead the AL in this category.

Yogi Berra had 7,546 career at-bats with the Yankees. He had more than 500 at-bats in seven of his 18 seasons in New York. He ranks fifth on New York's all-time career at-bat list: Derek Jeter (9,324), Mickey Mantle (8,102), Lou Gehrig (8,001) and Bernie Williams (7,869).

Dave Righetti had 46 saves in 1986, a team record for most saves in a season by a right-handed pitcher. This season total wouldn't be surpassed by any Yankee pitcher until Mariano Rivera recorded 50 saves in 2001.

Featured Figure

Yankee firsts at the new Yankee Stadium: game – April 16, 2009; win – 6-5 over Cleveland Indians on April 17; loss – 2-10 to the Cleveland Indians on April 16; pitch – ball thrown by CC Sabathia; batter – Derek Jeter; hit – single by Johnny Damon on April 16; run – Jorge Posada in fifth inning on April 16; home run – Jorge Posada in fifth inning on April 16; and error – Cody Ransom in sixth inning on April 16.

By The Numbers

••• ooo

New York Yankees

B
A
S
E
B
A
L
L

Babe Ruth had a slugging percentage of .847 in 1920, which stood as an Major League Baseball record for 81 years. It was broken by Barry Bonds in 2001. Ruth holds four of the top five seasons for slugging percentage in the American League, the other top season is held by Lou Gehrig (.765 in 1927).

New York had 47 home losses in 1908 and 1913, a team record for most home losses in a single-season.

New York celebrated "Babe Ruth Day" at Yankee Stadium on April 27, 1947. Other teams throughout MLB also celebrated the day in honor of the Yankee great.

The Yankees beat the Dodgers 4-3 in the 1947 World Series. Three games were decided by one run, with the Dodgers winning two. Spec Shea started three games for the Yankees, winning Games 1 and 5. He led all pitchers with a 2.35 ERA. This was the first of five seven game World Series wins for the Yankees.

Joe DiMaggio was named AL MVP in 1947, the third of his career. He had a .315 batting average and committed just one error for the season, the fewest of any Yankee MVP.

Featured Figure

Tommy Henrich hit a walk-off home run against the Dodgers in Game 1 of the 1949 World Series. The Yankees won the game 1-0 and the Series 4-1.

By The Numbers

New York Yankees

B
A
S
E

The Yankees retired Babe Ruth's jersey No. 3 on June 13, 1948. This marked the last time Ruth appeared at Yankee Stadium, he died two months later. The last Yankee to wear No. 3 was Cliff Mapes. He wore the number in 1948, then switched to another now retired number, No. 7.

B
A
L
L

Jack Chesbro was the starting pitcher in 51 games in 1904. He pitched complete games in 48 of them, a Yankee single-season record. The other top five seasons for complete games: Jack Powell (38 in 1904), Al Orth (36 in 1906), Jack Chesbro (33 in 1903) and Ray Caldwell (31 in 1915).

Derek Jeter has had 10,548 total plate appearances in his career, a New York record. He had 752 in 2005, a career single-season high. The rest of the top five on the career plate appearance list: Mickey Mantle (9,871), Lou Gehrig (9,660), Babe Ruth (9,198) and Bernie Williams (9,053).

The Yankees have played the Red Sox 2,030 times in the regular season, and lead the series 1,113-917 for a .548 winning percentage.

Ron Guidry recorded 248 strikeouts in 1978, a Yankee single-season record. The only other player to surpass 225 strikeouts in a season is Jack Chesbro (239 strikeouts in 1904).

By The Numbers

New York Yankees

**B
A
S
E
B
A
L
L**

Casey Stengel won 1,149 games as a Yankee manager. His overall record was 1,149-696 for a .623 winning percentage. The Yankees won 10 pennants and seven World Series titles under Stengel's time as manager. He was inducted into the Baseball Hall of Fame in 1966.

Babe Ruth's career batting average percentage was .349, a Yankee record. The rest in the top five: Lou Gehrig (.340), Earl Combs (.325), Joe DiMaggio (.325) and Derek Jeter (.314).

Lou Gehrig had 949 career RBIs at the old Yankee Stadium, a stadium record. The rest of the top five: Babe Ruth (777), Mickey Mantle (744), Yogi Berra (727) and Joe DiMaggio (720).

Lou Gehrig hit 49 home runs in 1934 and again in 1936, a team single-season record for home runs hit by a first baseman.

Yankee batters were walked 17 times in a game against the Washington Senators on Sept. 11, 1949, a team single-game record. Eleven batters were walked in the third inning, which is a team single-inning record.

Joe Page led Major League Baseball with 60 games pitched in 1949. He also led the American League with 55 games pitched in 1948.

By The Numbers

• • • ○○○

New York Yankees

B
A
S
E
B
A
L
L

The only time the Yankees have had two players hit 50 or more home runs in the same season was in 1961. Roger Maris had 61 home runs and Mickey Mantle had 54.

New York finished the season with 50 wins in 1912, a franchise record for fewest wins in a season.

Whitey Ford was 21 years old when he won the Series-clinching Game 4 of the 1950 World Series. The win made him the youngest Yankee pitcher to win a World Series game. Ford pitched eight scoreless innings before allowing two runs with two outs in the ninth inning.

Vic Raschi was called for balking four times against the White Sox on May 3, 1950, a team single-game record. Even so, he pitched a complete game and received the win after striking out eight and allowing 10 hits.

The Yankees swept the Philadelphia Phillies in the 1950 World Series. The first three games were decided by one run, and a three-run sixth inning in Game 4 gave the Yankees the needed lead to win the game 5-2. Vic Raschi pitched a complete game in Game 1 and allowed no earned runs. As a pitching staff, the Yankees had a 0.73 ERA.

Phil Rizzuto was named AL MVP in 1950. He had a .982 fielding percentage, the highest of his career.

By The Numbers

New York Yankees

ooo•••

B
A
S
E
B
A
L
L

Longtime Yankee Stadium public address announcer, Bob Sheppard, was considered "The Voice of Yankee Stadium" for many years. Sheppard announced his first game in 1951. He went on to announce more than 4,500 Yankee games in his distinguished career. When not working the booth, he made many cameo appearances in movies and TV shows, gave eulogies for many of our nation's icons (including former President Ronald Reagan), and even threw out the first pitch for a World Series game. In 2009 at age 99, he officially announced his intention to retire following the season. Not surprisingly, the Yankees renamed their media dining room "Sheppard's Place" in his honor. Interestingly, however, all of this almost never happened because he initially turned down the job due to scheduling conflicts with his original profession as a high school speech teacher. Sheppard passed away on July, 11, 2010, just three months before his 100th birthday.

The largest single-season attendance for Yankee home and road games was 7,325,051 in 2006.

New York used 51 players throughout the season in 2005 and 2008, a team record for most players used in a single season.

Gil McDougald was named American League Rookie of the Year in 1951. He played in 131 games and had 123 hits on 402 at-bats for a .306 batting average. He scored 72 times, recorded 63 RBIs and committed just 14 errors.

By The Numbers

•••ooo

New York Yankees

○ ○ ○ • • •

52

**B
A
S
E
B
A
L
L**

Babe Ruth was walked 1,852 times during his career as a Yankee, a team record. The rest of the top five: Mickey Mantle (1,733), Lou Gehrig (1,508), Bernie Williams (1,069) and Willie Randolph (1,005).

Derek Jeter has been hit by pitch 152 times in his career, a Yankee record. He was hit by pitch 14 times in 2004 and 2007, his single-season career high. The rest of the top five on the career list for most times hit by pitch: Frank Crosetti (114), Jason Giambi (109), Kid Elberfeld (81) and Alex Rodriguez (80).

Fritz Peterson had a career ERA of 2.52 at the old Yankee Stadium, the lowest among pitchers with 500 or more innings at the stadium. The rest of the top five: Whitey Ford (2.57), Mariano Rivera (2.61), Spud Chandler (2.62) and Stan Bahnsen (2.65).

The Yankees retired Joe DiMaggio's jersey No. 5 in 1952. He was elected to the Baseball Hall of Fame in 1955.

The Yankees beat the Brooklyn Dodgers 4-3 in the 1952 World Series. Mickey Mantle hit a home run in the sixth inning of Game 7 to break a 2-2 tie. A Mantle single in the seventh drove in Gil McDougald, and New York won the game 4-2. It was their fourth consecutive victory in World Series matchups against the Dodgers.

By The Numbers

• • • ○ ○ ○

New York Yankees

○○○●●●

BASEBALL

Mariano Rivera had 53 saves in 2004, the most saves in a season for any Yankee. He had 50 saves in 2001, and is the only Yankee to have recorded 50 or more saves in a season.

Don Mattingly led the team with 53 doubles in 1986, a single-season team record. Only Alfonso Soriano and Lou Gehrig have hit 50 or more doubles in a season. Gehrig hit 52 in 1927 and Soriano hit 51 in 2002.

New York batters grounded into double play 153 times in 1996, a team record for most in a single season. Nine players grounded into double play 10 or more times and Paul O'Neill led the team with 21.

The Yankee pitching staff allowed 753 earned runs in 2000, a team record for most in a season. David Cone led the team with 119 earned runs allowed.

Billy Martin drove in the winning run against the Dodgers in Game 6 of the 1953 World Series. The win won the Series and was the fifth consecutive championship for the Yankees.

Featured Figure

The New York Giants football team played home games at Yankee Stadium from 1956-73.

By The Numbers

●●●○○○

New York Yankees

54

**B
A
S
E
B
A
L
L**

Alex Rodriguez hit 54 home runs in 2007, a single-season Yankee record for a right-handed batter. He has hit 268 career home runs with the Yankees and currently ranks seventh on the all-time list. The rest of the top five on the list for most home runs in a season by a right-handed batter: Alex Rodriguez (48 in 2005), Joe DiMaggio (46 in 1937 and 39 in 1948) and Alfonso Soriano (39 in 2002).

Mickey Mantle hit 54 home runs in 1961, a single-season Yankee record for a switch-handed batter. He hit 536 career home runs with the Yankees and currently ranks second on the all-time list.

Babe Ruth hit 54 home runs in his first season with the Yankees, a team record for first year players with New York. He is followed on the list by Jason Giambi (41), Roger Maris (39) and Mark Teixeira (39).

The Yankees won 54 games on the road in 1939, a team record for most road wins in a season.

Bob Grim was named American League Rookie of the Year as a pitcher in 1954. He compiled a record of 20-6 for a .769 winning percentage. Grim allowed 175 hits, 78 runs and 72 earned runs in 199.0 innings pitched. He walked 85 batters and had a 3.26 ERA.

By The Numbers

New York Yankees

ooo•••

BASEBALL

The first black player to play for the Yankees was Elston Howard, who made the club in 1955. Howard went on to win two Gold Gloves and American League MVP in 1963. His jersey number was retired by the Yankees in 1984.

Jack Chesbro led Major League Baseball with 55 games pitched in 1904. He also led the league with 49 games pitched in 1906.

Jack Chesbro pitched 455.0 innings in 1904, the single-season Yankee record. Although this ranks 118th all-time in Major League Baseball history, he is one of only four MLB players to pitch for 400 or more innings in a season since 1900.

Whitey Ford led the American League with 18 wins in 1955. He is the first Yankee to lead the AL with less than 20 wins in a season.

Yogi Berra was named AL MVP in 1955, the third time he received the honor (1951 and 1954). Berra had 147 hits on 541 at-bats for a .272 average. He was the second catcher to have received the honor that began in 1922.

Featured Figure

Following home games at Yankee Stadium, the Frank Sinatra version of "New York, New York" is traditionally played. At one time the Liza Minnelli version was played after a loss.

By The Numbers

•••ooo

New York Yankees

B
A
S
E
B
A
L
L

Don Larsen is the only pitcher in major league history to throw a perfect game in the World Series. He accomplished this feat against the Brooklyn Dodgers in Game 5 of the 1956 Series. A rematch of the 1955 Series won by the Dodgers, Larsen caught the Dodgers' Dale Murphy looking to record the 27th out of the game. The Yankees won the Series in seven games.

Joe DiMaggio had a safe hit in 56 consecutive games in 1941, a Major League Baseball record. The streak began on May 15 and came to a close on July 17. The National League record is 48, set by Willie Keeler in 1897.

Whitey Ford is New York's career strikeout leader. He recorded 1,956 strikeouts as a Yankee from 1950, 1953-67. Second on the list is Andy Pettitte with 1,823 career strikeouts.

In May 1956 Mickey Mantle had a batting average of .414, hit 16 home runs and 35 RBIs. He is the only Yankee to have a batting average of .350 or better, hit 15 or more home runs and 35 or more home runs in a single month.

Mickey Mantle won the AL Triple Crown in 1956. He had 188 hits on 533 at-bats for a .353 batting average. He scored 132 runs and recorded 130 RBIs. Mantle had 22 doubles, five triples and led MLB with 52 home runs.

By The Numbers

• • • ○ ○ ○

New York Yankees

B
A
S
E
B
A
L
L

Babe Ruth recorded 457 total bases in 1921, a New York single-season record. Lou Gehrig and Joe DiMaggio are the only other Yankees to surpass 400 total bases in a season. Gehrig did it five times, Ruth twice and DiMaggio once.

Hank Bauer and Gil McDougald led the American League with nine triples each in 1957. This is the last time a Yankee has led the AL in triples. Overall, a Yankee has been the league leader 18 times starting with Wally Pipp in 1924. Earle Combs led the league three times (1927, 1928 and 1930), the most of any Yankee.

Tony Kubek was named AL Rookie of the Year in 1957. He played in 127 games and had 128 hits on 431 at-bats for a .297 batting average. He scored 56 times, recorded 39 RBIs and committed just 20 errors.

Mickey Mantle was named AL MVP in 1957, his second of three MVP Awards (1956 and 1962). He led Major League Baseball with 121 runs scored that season and had a .365 batting average, the highest season average of his career.

Featured Figure

George M. Steinbrenner High School, located in Lutz, Fla., north of Tampa Bay, opened in 2009. The school was named after the former Yankee owner to honor his many contributions to the community.

By The Numbers

New York Yankees

B
A
S
E
B
A
L
L

Fifty-eight Yankee pitchers have combined to hit 154 home runs since the first one was hit by Clark Griffith on July 14, 1903. Red Ruffing hit 30 career home runs, a team record amongst pitchers. Rounding out the top five on the career list are: Tommy Byrne (10), Spud Chandler (9), Don Larsen (8) and Mel Stottlemyre (7).

New York lost 58 road games in 1912, a team record for most road games lost in a season. The road record was 19-58 for a .247 winning percentage.

New York stranded 1,258 runners on base in 1996, a team record for most batters left on base in a season.

The Yankees beat the Milwaukee Braves 4-3 in the 1958 World Series. New York fell behind 1-3 after a loss in Game 4. But the Yankees rallied to beat the Braves 7-0 in Game 5, in extra innings in Game 6, and 6-2 in Game 7. Bob Turley was named World Series MVP. He pitched in four games, starting in two. Turley was the winning pitcher in Games 5 and 7. He also recorded a save in Game 6 and allowed just one run in 16 innings pitched over the deciding last three games of the Series.

Bob Turley won the Cy Young Award in 1958, the first Yankee to receive the honor. He had a record of 21-7, struck out 168, and allowed 178 hits in 245.1 innings pitched.

By The Numbers

• • • ○ ○ ○

New York Yankees

(59)

B A S E B A L L

Mariano Rivera has 559 career saves as a Yankee, the all-time career leader. Dave Righetti (224), Rich Gossage (151) and Sparky Lyle (141) follow Rivera on the all-time list and combine for 516 career saves. On the top ten list of most saves in a season, Rivera holds every spot but two. Righetti had 46 saves in 1986, which was good enough for the third best season. John Wetteland had 43 saves in 1996 and is tied for the fifth, with Rivera of course, for most saves in a season.

Babe Ruth holds the New York record for most career runs scored. Ruth scored 1,959 runs as a Yankee. The rest of the top five on the list: Lou Gehrig (1,888), Derek Jeter (1,686), Mickey Mantle (1,677) and Joe DiMaggio (1,390).

New York's career home-run record is held by Babe Ruth. He hit 659 home runs as a Yankee. He had more than 40 home runs in 11 seasons as a Yankee.

New York scored 459 runs in 1908, a team single-season record for fewest runs scored in a season. Charlie Hemphill led the team with 62 runs scored and was the only player with more than 50.

Yankee pitchers combined for 59 saves in 2004, the most in a season since the stat was first recorded in 1969. Mariano Rivera accounted for 53 of the 59.

By The Numbers

• • • ○ ○ ○

New York Yankees

60

B A S E B A L L

In the 1960 World Series against the Pirates, Bobby Richardson had a .367 batting average with 12 RBIs and only one strikeout over the seven game Series. The Yankees lost the Series 3-4 to the Pirates; however, Richardson was named MVP and is the only major league player to win the award on a losing team.

Yankee Stadium has always had much to offer fans – excitement, tradition, championships, and very large scoreboards. The first scoreboard in 1923 was large enough to show 12 innings of action for every major league baseball game. In 1959 a scoreboard with "message technology" was installed and was billed as the world's largest scoreboard. In 1974 yet another scoreboard was unveiled. This one had a length of 560 feet and was baseball's first-ever "telescreen." This scoreboard featured the innovative technology needed to show instant replays.

The letters over the main gate that spelled "Yankee Stadium" at the old stadium were originally white. They were painted blue sometime in the 1960s.

Bobby Richardson recorded a World Series record six RBIs against the Pirates in Game 3 of the 1960 Series.

Roger Maris led the American League with 112 RBIs in 1960. Maris also led the AL in RBIs in 1961 with 161 and is the last Yankee to lead the AL in this category for two seasons.

By The Numbers

• • • ○ ○ ○

New York Yankees

B
A
S
E
B
A
L
L

Roger Maris broke Babe Ruth's Major League Baseball single-season record of 60 home runs in the last game of the 1961 season. When the Yankees played the Red Sox on Oct. 1, Maris walked up to the plate in the bottom of the fourth with the score tied 0-0 and one out. With the first pitch, Maris hit a deep home run into right field off Red Sox pitcher Tracey Stallard, the only score for either team that afternoon. Maris' record of 61 home runs stood until 1998, when it was broken by Sammy Sosa (66) and Mark McGwire (70).

Red Ruffing pitched 261 complete games as a Yankee, a New York career record. He pitched a complete game in 66.8 percent of his 391 career starts. Ruffing played for the Yankees from 1930-46 and pitched 20 or more complete games in six seasons and less than 12 just twice, in 1945 (8) and 1946 (4).

Johnny Blanchard hit four pinch-hit home runs in 1961, a New York single-season record. The team combined for 10, which is also a single-season record.

Lou Gehrig had a team record .361 career-batting average in the postseason (min. 100 career postseason at-bats). He hit .545 in the 1928 World Series and .528 in the 1932 Series, both Yankee championship seasons.

By The Numbers

New York Yankees

**B
A
S
E
B
A
L
L**

The Yankee pitching staff pitched 1,506.2 innings in 1964, a team record for most innings pitched in a season. The top three pitchers that season: Jim Bouton (271.1), Whitey Ford (244.2) and Al Downing (244.0).

Bobby Richardson had 11 at-bats in a 22-inning game against the Detroit Tigers on June 24, 1962, a team record for most at-bats in a game. He had three hits for a .290 batting average and scored two runs. Seven other players in the game (three Yankees and four Tigers) had 10 at-bats.

Tom Thresh was named American League Rookie of the Year in 1962. He played in 157 games and had 178 hits on 622 at-bats for a .286 batting average. He scored 94 times, recorded 93 RBIs and committed just 20 errors.

The Yankees beat the San Francisco Giants 4-3 in the 1962 World Series. In Game 7, Roger Maris' fielding held Matty Alou at third base following a ninth-inning, two-out double hit by the Giants' Willie Mays. The Yankees recorded the last out in the next at-bat and won the game 1-0. Bill Skowron scored NY's only run from third base off Tony Kubek's connection with the ball in the fifth inning. It was the seventh matchup between the two franchises in the Series, but the first since the Giants left New York. Ralph Terry was named Series MVP with a 1.80 ERA over 25.0 innings pitched.

By
The
Numbers

•••ooo

New York Yankees

B
A
S
E
B
A
L
L

Hideki Matsui had an at-bat in 163 games in 2003, the Yankee record for most games with an at-bat in a season.

Lou Gehrig hit a Yankee record 163 triples during his career. The most he hit in a single-season was 20.

Andy Pettitte and Mariano Rivera have 63 all-time win-save combinations, the most in Major League Baseball history. Mike Mussina and Rivera are third on the all-time list with 49 win-save combinations.

Mariano Rivera has recorded 63 saves in interleague play, the most in Major League Baseball.

Babe Ruth led the American League with 163 runs scored in 1928. It was his third consecutive season leading the AL in runs and the seventh time of his Yankee career.

The Yankees were swept by the Los Angeles Dodgers in the 1963 World Series. It was only the second time in 40 Series appearances that the Yankees were swept. New York scored just four runs in the Series.

Joe McCarthy managed the Yankees from 1931-46. During his tenure, New York won eight AL Pennants and seven World Series titles (1932, 1936-39, 1941 and 1943). He led the Yankees to a postseason record of 29-9 for a .763 winning percentage, the highest postseason winning percentage of any Yankee manager.

By The Numbers

● ● ● ○ ○ ○

New York Yankees

B A S E B A L L

Miller Huggins managed the Yankees from 1918-29. In 1,786 games, he led the team to a record of 1,067-719 for a .597 winning percentage. New York won six American League Pennants and three World Series under Huggins. He was inducted into the Baseball Hall of Fame in 1964.

The Yankees had winning seasons every year from 1926 through 1964. The 39 consecutive winning seasons is a franchise record.

The Yankees played 164 regular-season games in 1964 and 1968, a team record for most games in the regular season.

Mickey Mantle hit a home run on each side of the plate against the Chicago White Sox on Aug. 12, 1964. It was the tenth switch-hit home run of his career, the most of any Yankee.

Waite Hoyt led the AL with a 2.64 ERA in 1927, the first Yankee pitcher to lead the AL in this category.

New York lost the 1964 World Series 3-4 to the Cardinals. The Yankees took a commanding lead in Game 6 after Joe Pepitone hit a grand slam in the eighth inning to tie the series 3-3. Down 3-7 in the ninth inning of Game 7, the Yankees hit two home runs (Clete Boyer and Phil Linz) but lost 5-7. It was the last World Series appearance for the Yankees for 12 years.

By The Numbers

● ● ● ○○○

New York Yankees

B A S E B A L L

Mickey Mantle hit .365 in 1957, a team single-season record for a switch hitter. He had 173 hits on 474 at-bats.

New York finished the 1961 season with a home record of 65-16 for a .802 winning percentage. This is the most home wins during a season in team history.

In 1965 Yankee pitchers struck out 1,001 batters, the first time the Yankee pitching staff surpassed 1,000 strikeouts. The top three pitchers had 155 or more strikeouts.

Opposing teams scored 165 times against Yankee pitcher Russ Ford in 1912, a team record. Ford also led the team in innings pitched with 291.2, for an average of .567 runs allowed per inning.

Bobby Richardson won his fifth straight Gold Glove Award in 1965. He is the only Yankee second baseman to have won the award.

Mickey Mantle hit a "tape measured" home run of 565 feet on April 17, 1953. The ball actually cleared the wall of the Washington Senators' Griffith Stadium, a first in stadium history.

Featured Figure

New York recorded its 5,000th win on Sept. 11, 1959, with a 9-3 victory against the Detroit Tigers.

By The Numbers

●●●ooo

New York Yankees

B A S E B A L L

All time, 171,676,866 fans have passed through the turnstiles for Yankee home games.

Yankee pitchers combined for a 2.66 ERA in 1917, a single-season record for lowest ERA since 1913. Ray Fisher's 2.19 ERA was the lowest among starting pitchers.

Mickey Mantle had 266 career home runs at the old Yankee Stadium, a stadium record. His total surpassed Babe Ruth's by seven. The rest of the top five: Lou Gehrig (251), Yogi Berra (210) and Joe DiMaggio (148).

The largest single-season attendance for Yankee road games was 3,308,666 in 2004. This is also a Major League Baseball record. The top five seasons for Yankee road games attracted more than 2.9 million fans.

Yankee players were walked 766 times in 1932, a team record for most bases-on-balls in a single season. Eight players were walked more than 50 times and two players were walked more than 100 times: Lou Gehrig (108) and Babe Ruth (130).

Yankee pitchers combined to strike out 1,266 batters in 2001, a team record for most strike outs by the pitching staff in a season. The top three pitchers with the most strikeouts that season: Andy Pettitte (164), Roger Clemens (213) and Mike Mussina (214).

By The Numbers

New York Yankees

B A S E B A L L

As Yankee manager, Joe McCarthy led New York to 1,460 regular-season wins. With only 867 losses and .627 winning percentage, McCarthy is the winningest manager in Yankee history. He was inducted into the Baseball Hall of Fame in 1957.

The Yankees scored 1,067 runs in 1931, a team single-season record for most runs scored. Seven players scored 100 or more runs for the season. Lou Gehrig led the team with 163 runs scored, which also led the American League.

Joe DiMaggio had 167 RBIs in 1937, a Yankee single-season record for right-handed batters. His next highest season total was 155 in 1948.

Lou Gehrig led Major League Baseball with 167 runs in 1936, his third time leading MLB and fourth time leading the American League in this category.

Featured Figure

With the Yankees trailing the Twins 9-12 in the bottom of the ninth on May 17, 2002, Jason Giambi hit a walk-off grand slam. It was only the second time a Yankee hit a walk-off grand slam with New York trailing by three runs. The first time was when Babe Ruth did it against the White Sox on Sept. 24, 1925, with the Yankees trailing 2-5 in the bottom of the tenth inning.

By The Numbers

● ● ● ○ ○ ○

New York Yankees

B A S E B A L L

The Yankees had a team batting average of .214 in 1968, the lowest in New York history. The team had 1,137 hits on 5,310 at-bats. Left fielder Roy White led the team with a .267 average. He was the only Yankee that season with an average above .250.

Stan Bahnsen was named the American League Rookie of the Year as a pitcher in 1968. He compiled a record of 17-12 for a .586 winning percentage. Bahnsen allowed 216 hits, 72 runs and 61 earned runs in 267.1 innings pitched. He walked 68 batters and had a 2.05 ERA.

Mickey Mantle led the Yankees with 18 home runs in 1968. It was only the second time since 1920 that the team home run leader had less than 20 home runs.

Jack Chesbro completed 168 games of his 227 career starts for .740 percent of starts completed. This is the highest among Yankee pitchers with 200 or more career starts.

Featured Figure

Some of the most fanatical Yankee fans can be found in section 203 at Yankee Stadium. Known as the "Bleacher Creatures," these fanatical fans do a roll call of Yankee players and perform a variety of humorous, sometimes vulgar, songs and chants.

By The Numbers

New York Yankees

B A S E B A L L

The Yankees recorded 69 errors in 2010, a single-season franchise low. Francisco Cervelli had 13 errors, the only player who committed more than 10 errors.

Ron Guidry recorded 969 strikeouts at the old Yankee Stadium, a stadium record. The rest of the top five: Andy Pettitte (816), Whitey Ford (748), Roger Clemens (710) and Mike Mussina (701).

Yankees were hit by pitch 14 times in 1969, a team record for fewest times hit by pitch in a season. Only two players were hit by pitch more than once: Bobby Murcer (3) and Frank Fernandez (3).

Yankee fans celebrated "Mickey Mantle Day" at Yankee Stadium on June 8, 1969. His jersey No. 7 was retired by New York that day, and he was elected to the Baseball Hall of Fame in 1974.

The longest 0-1 game lost by the Yankees was a 14-inning game against the Red Sox on Sept. 24, 1969. Boston's George Scott scored to win the game off a double hit by Mike Andrews.

Featured Figure

Nick Swisher is the last player to lead the team in batting average with an average of less than .300. Swisher led the Yankees in 2010 with a .288 batting average.

By The Numbers

New York Yankees

B
A
S
E
B
A
L
L

Babe Ruth was walked 170 times in 1923. This is still an American League single-season record. The rest of the top five seasons: Babe Ruth (150 in 1920), Mickey Mantle (146 in 1957) and Babe Ruth (145 in 1921 and 144 in 1926). Ruth also holds the spots from 6-9.

Casey Stengel's jersey No. 37 was retired by the Yankees in 1970, the only manager to have received the honor.

Whitey Ford pitched 3,170.1 innings with the Yankees, a team career record. He pitched 200 or more innings in 11 of his 16 seasons. Ford pitched 283.0 innings in 1961, his career single-season high. Number two on the career list for innings pitched is Red Ruffing. He pitched 3,168.2 innings with New York. Ruffing pitched 259.0 innings in 1932, his career single-season high.

Thurman Munson was named AL Rookie of the Year in 1970. He played in 132 games and had 137 hits on 453 at-bats for a .302 batting average. He scored 59 times, recorded 53 RBIs and committed just eight errors.

New York has played 16,760 regular-season games and has an all-time record of 9,552-7,208 for a .570 winning percentage.

Featured Figure

Yankee pitcher George Pipgras struck out five times in Game 3 of the 1932 World Series, a Major League Baseball record.

By The Numbers

● ● ● ○ ○ ○

New York Yankees

B A S E B A L L

The Yankees only hit 97 home runs as a team in 1971, the last time the team has failed to hit 100 or more home runs in a season. New York finished the season in fourth place in the division with a record of 82-80.

Yogi Berra recorded 71 hits in 75 World Series games. This is the Yankee career record for hits in the World Series.

Steve Sax hit 171 singles in 1989, a single-season record. He also led the team that season in hits (205), stolen bases (43) and batting average (.315).

Construction of the new Yankee stadium cost $1.5 billion, much higher than the $2.5 million construction cost for the original Yankee Stadium ($31.5 million in 2009 dollars). The first game at the new Yankee Stadium took place on April 16, 2009. Even though the Yankees lost 2-10 to the visiting Cleveland Indians that did not curb the enthusiasm of the 48,271 fans in attendance at their new home.

Yankee batters struck out 1,171 times in 2002, a team record for most strikeouts in a season. Five players struck out more than 100 times, and Alfonso Soriano led the team with 157 strikeouts.

Babe Ruth recorded 171 RBIs in 1921, the best single-season RBI total for a Yankee outfielder. This season total also ranks fourth best in New York history.

By The Numbers

New York Yankees

○○○ ••• ———————————————————— 72

B A S E B A L L

Lindy McDaniel hit a home run on Sept. 28, 1972. He is the last Yankee pitcher to hit a home run. It was the third and final home run of his career but his only one as a Yankee.

The Yankees retired jersey No. 8 in honor of Bill Dickey and Yogi Berra in 1972. Dickey caught more than 100 games in 13 consecutive seasons and did not allow a passed ball in 125 consecutive games, both AL records. Berra was inducted into the Baseball Hall of Fame in 1972. He played in 2,120 regular season games with the Yankees and had a .285 career batting average. The two catchers combined for 3,873 career games and 2,104 runs scored.

Bobby Murcer led the American League with 102 runs scored in 1972. This is the lowest run total for a Yankee who has led the AL in runs scored. He also led the team in batting average (.292), hits (171), doubles (30), triples (7), home runs (33) and RBIs (96). He is the only player to be the sole leader in all of these categories in a season.

Featured Figure

New York and Boston tied for first atop the division in 1978 and the two teams met for a one-game playoff on Oct. 2. Trailing 0-2 in the seventh inning, Bucky Dent hit a three-run home run over Boston's "Green Monster." The home run was only Dent's fifth of the season, but it was enough to help the Yankees to a 5-4 victory.

By The Numbers

••• ○○○

New York Yankees

B
A
S
E
B
A
L
L

A group headed by George Steinbrenner bought the Yankees from CBS in 1973 for $8.7 million after New York failed to win a pennant for eight straight seasons. Adjusted for inflation, the amount paid for the team was equal to $42.7 million in 2010. Forbes magazine estimated the value of the Yankees franchise at $1.6 billion in 2010.

Jason Giambi was the Yankees designated hitter in 373 games during the 2000s, the most of any player. He is followed by Hideki Matsui (252) and Bernie Williams (120).

Ron Bloomberg was the first Yankee to enter the starting lineup as a designated hitter on April 6, 1973. He hit a single in the top of the third inning. The American League adopted the designated hitter rule in 1973.

Featured Figure

Oakland took a 2-0 lead over the Yankees in the 2001 American League Division Series. With the Yankees holding a narrow 1-0 lead, Derek Jeter flipped the ball to Jorge Posada to tag out Jason Giambi at home for the last out of the seventh inning. The Yankees won the game, and Jeter's throw became known as "The Flip Play." New York won the series but eventually lost to the Diamondbacks in the World Series.

By The Numbers

● ● ● ○ ○ ○

New York Yankees

B
A
S
E
B
A
L
L

Ron Guidry set the Yankee single-season record for lowest ERA for left-handed pitchers in 1978. He had a 1.74 ERA in his Cy Young Award winning season.

Fritz Maisel led Major League Baseball with 74 stolen bases in 1914. He was caught stealing just 17 times. Maisel was the first Yankee to lead the league in this category.

Derek Jeter had 1,274 career hits at the old Yankee Stadium, a stadium record. His total surpassed Lou Gehrig's by five hits. The rest of the top five: Mickey Mantle (1,211), Bernie Williams (1,123) and Joe DiMaggio (1,060).

Yankee managers are 62-45 all-time on opening day for a .574 winning percentage.

Jim Mason hit four doubles against the Rangers on July 8, 1974, tying a single-game team record originally set by Johnny Lindell on Aug. 17, 1944.

On Dec. 31, 1974, Jim "Catfish" Hunter became the first free agent signed by the Yankees. New York signed him to a $3 million contract for five years.

Featured Figure

New York recorded its 1,000th win on Sept. 9, 1909, with a 4-1 victory against the Philadelphia Athletics.

By The Numbers

New York Yankees

**B
A
S
E
B
A
L
L**

The Yankees bought Babe Ruth's contract from the Boston Red Sox in 1919 for $475,000. Boston received $125,000 in cash and a $350,000 loan in the exchange that changed baseball history.

Lou Gehrig participated in fielding 1,575 double plays during his career, a team career record. He is followed on the career list by: Don Mattingly (1,504), Willie Randolph (1,233), Derek Jeter (1,226) and Phil Rizzuto (1,217).

Jim "Catfish" Hunter pitched 30 complete games for the Yankees in 1975. No player in Major League Baseball has thrown as many complete games in a season since.

Jim "Catfish" Hunter led the American League with 23 wins and 328.0 innings pitched in 1975.

Lou Gehrig led Major League Baseball with 175 RBIs in 1927.

The Yankees pitching staff recorded 20 saves in 1975, the last time the team had less than 30 saves in a season.

Featured Figure

In 1956, the Yankees began awarding the James P. Dawson Award to the top rookie in spring training camp in honor of a popular New York Times sports reporter who covered the Yankees. Outfielder Jon Weber won the award in 2010.

By The Numbers

• • • ○○○

New York Yankees

B
A
S
E
B
A
L
L

New York has been swept in the World Series three times, by the New York Giants in 1922, Los Angeles Dodgers in 1963 and Cincinnati Reds in 1976.

New York holds spring training in Tampa at their Advanced A affiliate facility, which is known as the Yankees' Steinbrenner Field. Total seating at the stadium is 11,076, making it the largest stadium in the Grapefruit League. The Yankees have held spring training in Tampa since 1996.

Ron Guidry had 176 strikeouts in 1977, the most single-season strikeouts by a rookie since 1950. The rest of the top five: Al Downing (171), Stan Bahnsen (162), Doc Medich (145) and Orlando Hernandez (131).

Thurman Munson became the team's honorary captain prior to the start of the 1976 season. He was the first player to hold the position since Lou Gehrig. He held the position until his death in a private plane accident on Aug. 2, 1979.

Chris Chambliss was the first Yankee batter in the bottom of the ninth inning of Game 5 of the 1976 American League Championship Series. With the game tied 6-6, Chambliss hit a walk-off home run on the first pitch to give the Yankees their 30th AL Pennant, the team's first since 1964.

By The Numbers

• • • ○ ○ ○

New York Yankees

B
A
S
E
Babe Ruth scored 177 times in 1921, a Yankee single-season record. He scored 150 or more runs five other seasons during his career. Lou Gehrig scored 150 or more runs in a season twice and Joe DiMaggio did it once. These three are the only Yankees to have accomplished this feat.

B
A
L
Bob Turley walked 177 batters in 1955, a team single-season record for right-handed pitchers. Turley also led the starting rotation in the most earned runs (84) and strikeouts (210).

L
Sparky Lyle replaced Mike Torrez with two outs in the eighth inning of Game 5 of the 1977 American League Championship Series with the Yankees trailing the Royals 2-3. Lyle struck out Cookie Rojas to end the inning and the Yankees scored three in the ninth to take a 5-3 lead. Lyle allowed one hit in the ninth, but no runs. The win was Lyle's second in two nights after pitching 5.1 scoreless innings to finish out Game 4.

The Yankees beat the Los Angeles Dodgers 4-2 in the 1977 World Series. Despite outscoring the Yankees 24-18 in the first five games, the Dodgers needed to win the final three in the Series. Reggie Jackson hit a two-run home run in the fourth inning of Game 6 to put the Yankees up for good. But he wasn't done. Jackson hit a two-run home run in the fifth and a single home run in the eighth. His spectacular performance led to a Series MVP.

By The Numbers

New York Yankees

B
A
S
E
B
A
L
L

Mariano Rivera has pitched in 978 career games as a Yankee, a team record. He has pitched in 60 or more games in a season 13 times in his career. The rest of the top five on the list of career games pitched: Dave Righetti (522), Whitey Ford (498), Mike Stanton (456) and Red Ruffing (426).

Ron Guidry is the only Yankee Cy Young Award recipient to be a unanimous selection. He won the award in 1978 with a 25-3 record and a 1.74 ERA.

Don Mattingly had 1,378 putouts in 1986, the most in the American League. It was the eleventh time a Yankee has led the AL in putouts: Hal Chase (1911), Wally Pipp (1915, 1919 and 1920), Lou Gehrig (1927 and 1928), Babe Dahlgren (1940), Bill Skowron (1960), Joe Pepitone (1964 and 1969).

Ron Guidry recorded nine shutouts in 1978, a team single- season record. He is followed on the list by: Russ Ford (8), Whitey Ford (8) and five seasons of seven shutouts by various pitchers.

The Yankees beat the Dodgers 4-2 in the 1978 World Series. Buck Dent was named MVP. He recorded 10 hits on 24 at bats for a .417 average over the Series, the highest among all Yankees. The win would be New York's last Series title for 18 years.

By The Numbers

• • • ○ ○ ○

New York Yankees

**B
A
S
E
B
A
L
L**

Babe Ruth's career on-base percentage was .479, a Yankee record. Lou Gehrig is second on the list with a .442 career on-base percentage. The rest of the top five: Mickey Mantle (.422), Charlie Keller (.408) and Jason Giambi (.404).

Tommy Byrne walked 179 batters in 1949, a team single-season record. Byrne also led the starting rotation in fewest hits allowed (125), fewest earned runs (84), fewest home runs allowed (11) and most strikeouts (129).

Mike Stranton pitched in 79 games in 2002, a New York single-season record for a left-handed pitcher. Stranton had a 3.00 ERA that season, the lowest amongst all the closing pitchers.

Ron Guidry led the American League in 1979 with a 2.78 ERA. It was his second consecutive season leading the AL in this category.

Lou Gehrig had 220 hits on 581 at-bats in 1930 for a .379 batting average, the best single-season average for a Yankee first baseman.

Featured Figure

Tim Leary set the Yankee single-season record for wild pitches with 23 in 1990. Not surprisingly, he also led the team that year in times hitting a batter (7).

By The Numbers

• • • ○ ○ ○

New York Yankees

80

B
A
S
E

Babe Ruth's salary was $80,000 for each of the 1930 and 1931 seasons, the highest annual salary during his career. Adjusted for inflation, the 1931 contract is valued at $1.15 million in 2010 dollars. In comparison, the league minimum salary was $400,000 in 2010 and Alex Rodriguez was paid $33 million.

B
A
L
L

Dick Howser managed the Yankees to a 103-60 record (.632) in the 1980 regular season, the highest winning percentage of any manager that lasted one season or less. His regular-season success did not transfer into the postseason. The Yankees were swept in the American League Championship Series by the Kansas City Royals.

In 1980 Joe Lefebvre hit a home run against Toronto on May 22 and May 23. He is the only Yankee to hit a home run in his first two Major League Baseball games.

The Yankees played 6,580 games at the old Yankee Stadium. New York had an all-time record of 4,133-2,430-17 at the stadium for a .629 winning percentage.

CBS bought 80 percent of the Yankee franchise in for $11.2 million following the end of the 1964 season.

The Yankees signed Dave Winfield as a free agent on Dec. 15, 1980. He played for the Yankees from 1981-88 and part of the 1990 season. Winfield won five Gold Glove Awards as a Yankee.

By The Numbers

• • • ○ ○ ○

New York Yankees

B
A
Original distance to the left-field foul pole measured 281 feet. That distance increased throughout the years until it settled at 318 feet in 1988.

S
E
B
New York played 1,481 games in the 1910s. The Yankees record for the decade was 701-780 for a .473 winning percentage. This is the only decade that New York finished under .500.

A
L
L
Joe DiMaggio had a .381 batting average in 1939, the Yankee single-season record for a right-handed batter. He had 176 hits on 462 at-bats. Four other players hit .300 or better that season.

Graig Nettles was named MVP of the 1981 American League Championship Series against the Athletics with a .500 batting average and nine RBIs.

Yankee batters were hit by pitch 81 times in 2003, a team record for most times hit by pitch as a team in a season.

Alfonso Soriano recorded 381 total bases in 2002, making him the first Yankee second baseman to surpass 360 in a season.

Featured Figure

Stan Bahnsen was named AL Rookie of the Year as a pitcher in 1968. He compiled a record of 17-12 for a .586 winning percentage. Bahnsen allowed 216 hits, 72 runs and 61 earned runs in 267.1 innings pitched. He walked 68 batters and had a 2.05 ERA.

By The Numbers

•••○○○

New York Yankees

○ ○ ○ • • •

**B
A
S
E
B
A
L
L**

Robinson Cano had 482 assists in 2008, the most in the American League. It was the tenth time a Yankee has led the AL in putouts: Roger Peckinpaugh (1918), Del Pratt (1919 and 1920), Everett Scott (1922), Frankie Crosetti (1938), Joe Gordon (1939 and 1940), Phil Rizzuto (1952) and Derek Jeter (1997).

Yankee base runners were caught stealing 82 times in 1920, a team record for most times in a season. Five players were caught 10 or more times. Babe Ruth and Ping Bodie led the team with 14 times.

The Yankees allowed 182 home runs in 2004, a team record for most allowed in a season.

Featured Figure

The most recognizable sports logos in the world is arguably the interlocking N and Y of the New York Yankees. The first use of the logo was not for the Yankees or any other sports team for that matter. It was designed by Louis B. Tiffany in 1877 as a medal for New York City police officer John McDowell, the first city police officer shot in the line of duty. Yankee owner Bill Devery, a former NYC police chief, may have been the driving force in introducing the logo to the Yankees uniform. Interestingly, the logo was removed from the jersey from 1917-36. And one of the greatest players to ever put on a Yankees uniform, Babe Ruth, never even wore a jersey with this trademark insignia.

By The Numbers

• • • ○ ○ ○

New York Yankees

B A S E B A L L

The Yankees had 1,683 hits as a team in 1930, a single-season franchise record. Eight players had 100 or more hits: Lou Gehrig (220), Babe Ruth (186), Earle Combs (183), Tony Lazzeri (173), Ben Chapman (162), Lyn Lary (134), Bill Dickey (124) and Harry Rice (103). The combined hits of these eight players are more than the team total for 20 different seasons.

Yogi Berra threw out the first ceremonial pitch at the new Yankee Stadium. Yankee catcher Jose Molina had the honor of catching the pitch thrown by the then 83-year old Yankee Hall of Famer.

Dave Righetti struck out Boston's Wade Boggs on July 4, 1983, to record the Yankees' first regular-season no-hitter since 1951. Righetti recorded nine strikeouts and walked four batters.

The Yankees and Royals played in the "Pine Tar" game on July 24, 1983. George Brett of the Royals hit a ninth-inning home run to give Kansas City a 5-4 lead. However, he was called out after a decision by the umpire that the tar on his bat exceeded above the allowed 18 inches. A reversal was made following the game and it was resumed three weeks later at the point after Brett's ejection. Kansas City ultimately won the game 5-4.

By The Numbers

New York Yankees

B
A
S
E
B
A
L
L

Lou Gehrig recorded 184 RBIs in 1931, a New York single-season record. Gehrig holds the top three spots for most RBIs in a season by a Yankee and five of the top nine.

Original plans for old Yankee Stadium called for a third deck and for the stands to fully wrap around the field, which would have increased capacity to around 100,000.
However, these plans were ultimately scaled back. White Construction Co. signed the contract for $2.5 million and completed the project in just 284 working days.

The Yankees had 6,584 total chances in 1916, a single-season team record. Five players had more than 450 chances and Wally Pipp led the team with 1,625.

Don Mattingly recorded 207 hits on 603 at-bats for a .343 batting average in 1984. It was the first time since 1962 that a Yankee recorded 200 or more hits in a season.

Ron Guidry and Dave Winfield won Gold Glove Awards in 1984, the third consecutive year as the only Yankees to win the award.

Featured Figure

The Yankees played the St. Louis Cardinals in the 1926 World Series, the first against a team other than the New York Giants. The Yankees lost the Series 3-4.

By The Numbers

New York Yankees

BASEBALL

The Yankees had three Gold Glove Award winners in 1985: Ron Guidry, Don Mattingly and Dave Winfield. This is the most Yankees selected in a season for the award.

Derek Jeter has 185 career hits in the postseason, a Major League Baseball record. He recorded at least one hit in every postseason series. Second on the all-time MLB list is Bernie Williams. Williams had 128 career postseason hits and had 10 or more hits in three of his 25 postseason series appearances.

The Yankees are 144-102 in interleague play for a .585 winning percentage. New York finished 5-10 in interleague play in 1997, the only season with a losing record.

Don Baylor was hit by pitch 24 times in 1985, a single-season team record. The next highest on the team that season was five.

Yankee fans celebrated "Phil Rizzuto Day" at Yankee Stadium on Aug. 4, 1985, when New York retired Rizzuto's jersey No. 10. During his 13 seasons with the Yankees (1941-56), Rizzuto led the American League in: fielding percentage (1950), assists (1952), putouts (1942 and 1950), sacrifice hits (1949-52) and singles (1950). He had a career batting average of .273 and was named AL MVP in 1950. He was elected to the Baseball Hall of Fame in 1994.

By The Numbers

New York Yankees

B
A
S
E
B
A
L
L

The Yankees committed 386 team errors in 1912, a single-season team record. Seven players committed 20 or more errors. Jack Martin led the team with 42 errors. New York finished the season 50-102.

Paul Quantrill pitched in 86 games in 2004, a Yankee single-season record. Only two other players have pitched in 80 or more games in a season: Scott Proctor in 2006 (83) and Tom Gordon in 2004 (80).

Herb Pennock pitched 286.0 innings in 1924, the Yankee single-season record for a left-handed pitcher. His 2.83 ERA led the team that season.

New York had 2,086 assists in 1904, a team single-season record. Six players had more than 100 and Jimmy Williams led the team with 465.

Don Mattingly recorded 24 consecutive safe-hits in 1986, the eighth longest streak in New York history. Only one player has had a longer hitting streak since 1943 – Derek Jeter's streak of 25 in 2006.

Butch Wynegar caught 57 games for the Yankees in 1986, the fewest games caught by the season leader in Yankee history. Other catchers used that season: Ron Hassey, Joel Skinner and Juan Espino.

By The Numbers

• • • ○ ○ ○

New York Yankees

○ ○ ○ • • •

B
A
S
E
B
A
L
L

The total seating capacity at Yankee Stadium is 50,287. Old Yankee Stadium had a capacity of 56,886. The new stadium has wider seats and more legroom.

Don Mattingly hit six grand slams in 1987, a single-season team record. Mattingly never hit a grand slam before or after the 1987 season.

The Yankees hit 10 grand slams as a team in 1987, a team record for grand slams in a season.

New York players combined for a slugging percentage of .287 in 1914, a team record for lowest in a season. Birdie Cree led the team with a .411 slugging percentage, the only one player with a percentage higher than .330.

Don Mattingly hit a home run in eight consecutive games in 1987, a team record.

The Yankees had 1,487 assists in 2000, a team record for fewest in a season. Only two players had more than 200, Scott Brosius with 231 and Derek Jeter with 349.

Featured Figure

The only World Series the Yankees lost in eight appearances under manager Joe McCarthy was in 1942. New York lost the Series in five games. The Yankees lost just five games in seven Series wins under McCarthy.

By The Numbers

• • • ○ ○ ○

New York Yankees

**B
A
S
E
B
A
L
L**

Billy Martin managed the Yankees for the last time in 1988. He had five tenures as Yankee manager (1975-78, 1979, 1983, 1985 and 1988). He led the Yankees to a record of 556-385 for a .591 winning percentage. New York won two American League Pennants and one World Series under Martin. His jersey No. 1 was retired in 1986, mainly for his days as a player from 1950-56. He was a solid postseason player, with a batting average of .333 in 28 World Series games in the early 1950s.

Yankee pitchers combined for a 4.88 ERA in 1930, a single-season record for the highest ERA since 1913. George Pipgras' 4.11 ERA was the lowest among starting pitchers. Babe Ruth pitched nine innings and his 3.00 ERA was the lowest among all players that pitched at least one inning.

No Yankee won a Silver Slugger Award in 1988, the first time since the award began in 1980. It was the first of five consecutive seasons without a Yankee winner. The award has been given to a Yankee 36 times since its inception.

Rickey Henderson stole 93 bases in 1988, a team single-season record. The rest of the top five best seasons: Henderson (87 in 1986 and 80 in 1985), Fritz Maisel (74 in 1914) and Ben Chapman (61 in 1931).

By The Numbers

● ● ● ○ ○ ○

New York Yankees

B
A
S
E
B
A
L
L

Don Larsen threw just 89 pitches in his 1956 World Series perfect game – 26 balls, 44 strikes and 19 infield outs. He threw 15 pitches in the first inning, the most of any inning. He had four innings with fewer than 10 pitches. Pee Wee Reese was the only Dodger to get more than two balls on Larsen. He reached a full count in the first inning before getting caught looking.

New York players combined for a slugging percentage of .489 in 1927, a team record for highest in a season. Six players had a percentage higher than .500. Babe Ruth led the team with a percentage of .772, edging out Lou Gehrig's .765.

The Yankees stole 289 bases in 1910, a team record for most in a season. Six players had more than 20 stolen bases and Bert Daniels led the team with 41.

Featured Figure

Yankee firsts at the old Yankee Stadium: game – April 18, 1923; win – 4-1 over Red Sox in first game; loss – 3-4 to the Washington Senators on April 22; pitch – ball thrown by Bob Shawkey; batter – Whitey Whit; hit – single by Aaron Ward on April 18; run – Bob Shawkey in third inning on April 18; home run – Babe Ruth in third inning on April 18; and error – Babe Ruth in fifth inning on April 18.

By The Numbers

New York Yankees

B
A
S
E
B
A
L
L

Original distance to center field measured 490 feet. This dropped to 461 feet in 1937 following stadium renovations, which included the addition of a third deck to the right-field stands and the replacement of wooden bleachers with sturdier concrete seats.

Lou Gehrig holds the Yankee record for extra-base hits in a career. He recorded 1,190 career extra-base hits, one more than Babe Ruth. He hit 117 in 1927, a single-season high for his career. The rest of the top five on career extra-base hits: Mickey Mantle (952), Joe DiMaggio (881) and Bernie Williams (791).

Lefty Gomez threw 1,090 balls in 2,498.1 innings pitched during his career, the team record for balls thrown in a career. The most balls thrown in one season by Gomez was 122 in 1936. Only two other players have thrown more than 1,000 balls in their career: Red Ruffing (1,066) and Whitey Ford (1,086).

Red Ruffing led the American League with 190 strikeouts in 1932. It was the first time a Yankee led the AL in strikeouts. Ruffing was followed in this accomplishment by: Lefty Gomez (1933, 1934 and 1937), Vic Raschi (1951), Allie Reynolds (1952) and Al Downing (1964).

New York finished in last place in 1990, the first time since 1966 and only the fifth time in Yankee history.

By The Numbers

••• ○○○

New York Yankees

BASEBALL

New York batters grounded into double play 91 times in 1963, a team record for fewest in a single season. Eight players grounded into double play five or more times and Elston Howard led the team with 17.

Joe Girardi is the 32nd manager in Yankee history. His first season was in 2008. Girardi has led the Yankees to a record of 287-199 for a .591 winning percentage, one American League Pennant, and one World Series Championship.

Derek Jeter tied Lou Gehrig's Yankee all-time hit record in the seventh inning against the Tampa Bay Rays on Sept. 9, 2009. Although Jeter achieved this record in 46 fewer games, he had 588 more at-bats than Gehrig. Gehrig had 8,001 at-bats compared to Jeter's 8,589. Jeter surpassed Gehrig in his 8,591st at-bat in his 2,120th game on Sept. 11, 2009. The record-breaking single to right field came at Yankee Stadium in the third inning off Baltimore Orioles pitcher Chris Tillman.

Lou Piniella had 3,291 at-bats in 1,037 games as a Yankee from 1974-84. He had 971 hits for a .295 average.

Featured Figure

Mariano Rivera has a career ERA of 2.23, the best of any Yankee pitcher. Rivera had an ERA below 2.00 in 10 of his 16 seasons. Only two seasons was his ERA above 2.85 (5.51 in 1995 and 3.15 in 2007).

By The Numbers

● ● ● ○ ○ ○

New York Yankees

○ ○ ○ • • •

B
A
S
E
B
A
L
L

Derek Jeter was selected as New York's first pick, sixth overall, in the 1992 Major League Baseball Draft. Jeter was drafted out of Kalamazoo Central H.S. in Michigan.

The last time the Yankees failed to go .500 for the season was in 1992. The team finished with a 76-86 record for a .469 winning percentage.

The Yankees played in four consecutive extra-inning games in 1992, a team record. The Yankees finished 2-2 in those games.

Bobby Richardson set the team record for at-bats with 692 in 1962. The record stood for 40 years until broken by Alfonso Soriano's 696 at-bats in 2002. The other top five at-bat season totals: Horace Clarke (686 in 1970), Alfonso Soriano (682 in 2003) and Bobby Richardson (679 in 1964).

The most times a Yankee has grounded into double play in a single game is three. This has happened three times, most recently by Matt Nokes against the Twins on May 3, 1992.

Featured Figure

The Yankees have put together a string of consecutive World Series Championships six times. The five consecutive Series titles from 1949-53 is a Major League Baseball record.

By The Numbers

• • • ○ ○ ○

New York Yankees

B
A
S
E
B
A
L
L

Ron Guidry's .893 winning percentage (25-3) in 1978 is a single-season team record. He started the season 13-0 before getting his first loss on July 7 against the Brewers.

Babe Ruth had a .393 batting average in 1923, a team single-season record. He had 205 hits on 522 at-bats. Yankee players have hit .375 or better in a season just six times in franchise history. Ruth accomplished this feat four times (1921-24), Lou Gehrig once (1930) and Joe DiMaggio once (1939).

The Yankees recorded just 3,993 putouts in 1935, a team record for fewest in a season. Lou Gehrig led the team with 1,337. Bill Dickey had the second most on the team with 536.

Jim Abbott pitched a no-hitter against the Cleveland Indians on Sept. 4, 1993, the seventh in Yankee history. He struck out three batters and walked five. Abbott threw 66 strikes on 119 pitches.

Featured Figure

Alex Rodriguez hit 26 home runs at the old Yankee Stadium in 2005 and again in 2007. This is the team single-season record for home runs by a right-handed batter in the stadium.

By The Numbers

New York Yankees

B
A
S
E
B
A
L
L

The largest non-opening day attendance for a game at the remodeled old Yankee Stadium (1976-2008) was 56,294 on June 6, 1999, against the Mets.

The Yankee pitching staff recorded two shutouts in 1994, a team record for fewest shutouts pitched in a single season.

The Yankee pitching staff allowed 394 earned runs in 1904, a team record for fewest allowed in a season. Jack Powell led the team with 106 earned runs allowed in 390.1 innings pitched.

Whitey Ford holds the World Series record with 94 career strikeouts. He also holds the record for 33 career scoreless innings in World Series games.

Paul O'Neill was American League Batting Champion in 1994. He had 132 hits on 368 at-bats for a .359 batting average. He scored 68 runs and recorded 83 RBIs. O'Neill had 25 doubles, one triple and 21 home runs. These totals are from a strike-shortened season of 113 games.

Yankee pitchers combined for five wild pitches against the Cleveland Indians on June 24, 1994, a team single-game record. New York won the game 11-6.

By The Numbers

New York Yankees

○○○ ● ● ●

**B
A
S
E
B
A
L
L**

Original distance to the right-field foul pole at the old Yankee Stadium measured 295 feet. That distance moved up many times before settling at 314 feet in 1988.

Lou Gehrig recorded 1,995 RBIs during his career, a Yankee record. Only three other Yankees have recorded 1,500 or more career RBIs: Babe Ruth (1,976), Joe DiMaggio (1,537) and Mickey Mantle (1,509).

Mariano Rivera made his pitching debut with the Yankees on May 23, 1995. He was the starting pitcher and was pulled in the fourth inning after walking three and allowing five earned runs off eight hits.

Red Ruffing allowed 2,995 hits during his career with the Yankees, a team record. Ruffing allowed 219 hits on 259 innings pitched in 1932 for a .846 hit per inning average, the lowest single-season average of his career. He only allowed more than one hit per inning pitched in three of his 17 seasons.

New York recorded 995 RBIs in 1936, a single-season team record. Five players recorded 107 or more RBIs for the season. Lou Gehrig led the team with 152 RBIs.

Jim Leyritz hit a two-run home run in the 15th inning of Game 2 of the 1995 American League Division Series to give the Yankees a 7-5 victory over the Seattle Mariners. It was the longest postseason game in Yankee history.

By The Numbers

● ● ● ○○○

New York Yankees

○ ○ ○ • • • ─────────────────────

B
A
S
E
B
A
L
L

Jeter was named American League Rookie of the Year in 1996, the most recent Yankee and the fifth of all time to win the award. For the season, Jeter played in 157 games, had 183 hits on 582 at-bats for a .314 batting average, and recorded 78 RBIs. His fielding percentage was .969, with 244 putouts and 444 assists. Other players to win the AL Rookie of the Year Award are Gil McDougald (1951), Tony Kubek (1957), Tom Tresh (1962) and Thurman Munson (1970). The following won the award as pitchers: Bob Grim (1954), Stan Bahnsen (1968) and Dave Righetti (1981).

Don Mattingly hit 96 career sacrifice fly balls, a Yankee record. The most he hit in a single-season was 15 in 1986. This stat was first recorded in 1954.

Don Mattingly had a career-fielding percentage of .996, highest among all Yankees that played in 1,000 or more career games. Mattingly had 14,270 career putouts, 1,121 assists and only 68 errors.

Bernie Williams was named MVP of the 1996 American League Championship Series against the Baltimore Orioles. He hit a walk-off home run in the 11th inning of Game 1 and had a .474 batting average for the series.

Bernie Williams hit a switch-hit home run against the Rangers in the 1996 AL Division Series. This was the second of his career.

By The Numbers

• • • ○ ○ ○

New York Yankees

B A S E B A L L

The first regular-season game between the Yankees and Mets took place at Yankee Stadium on June 16, 1997. The Yankees lost the first interleague matchup 0-6, but lead the overall series 47-33 for a .588 winning percentage. Since 1997, the Yankees have lost the annual series twice, in 2004 and 2008.

CC Sabathia is the last Yankee to lead the team in strikeouts, wins, innings pitched and ERA. In 2009 Sabathia had 197 strikeouts, 19 wins, 230.0 innings pitched, and had a 3.37 ERA. He is the 18th Yankee to accomplish this feat.

Mariano Rivera has led the team in saves every year since 1997, accumulating 554 saves during that period. John Wetteland led the team with 43 saves in 1996, Rivera had five saves that season.

Roger Peckinpaugh had 360 errors over 1,214 career games played as a Yankee for .297 errors per game. This is the highest error-per-game average among players with 1,000 or more games played. The rest of the top five on the list: Frank Crosetti, 421 errors, 1,658 games, .297 errors per game; Hal Chase, 260 errors, 1,059 games, .246 errors per game; Joe Gordon, 192 errors, 1,000 games, .192 errors per game; and Tony Lazzeri, 297 errors, 1,649 games, .180 errors per game.

By The Numbers

New York Yankees

○○○••• —————————————————— **98**

**B
A
S
E
B
A
L
L**

In 1998 Bernie Williams led the American League with a .339 batting average. This has been accomplished nine other times by Yankees: Babe Ruth (.378 in 1924), Lou Gehrig (.363 in 1934), Joe DiMaggio (.381 in 1939 and .352 in 1940), Snuffy Stirnweiss (.309 in 1945), Mickey Mantle (.353 in 1956), Don Mattingly (.343 in 1984) and Paul O'Neill (.359 in 1994).

The largest single-game attendance at the remodeled old Yankee Stadium (1976-2008) was 56,717 for opening day against the Oakland A's on April 10, 1998. This beat the previous record by just seven attendees, which was set on opening day the previous season, also against the A's.

David Wells was named the American League Championship Series MVP in 1998, the first Yankee pitcher to receive the honor. Other Yankee pitchers to receive the award: Orlando Hernandez (1999), Andy Pettitte (2001), Mariano Rivera (2003) and CC Sabathia (2009).

New York won 114 games in 1998, a team record for the most wins in a season. The team finished with a 114-48 record for a .704 winning percentage. The win total is a single-season American League record.

The Yankees had 10 players with 10 or more home runs in 1998, a team record for most players with double-digit home runs in a season. Tino Martinez led the team with 28 home runs.

By The Numbers

•••○○○

New York Yankees

B
A
S
E
B
A
L
L

The Yankees played the Red Sox in the 1999 American League Championship Series, the first meeting of the teams in the postseason. New York won the series 4-1 and the two teams have since met two other times in the American League Championship Series. The Yankees won the second series matchup 4-3 in 2003 and lost the third 3-4 in 2004.

Seventeen Yankee batters struck out in a game against the Red Sox on Sept. 10, 1999, a single-game team record. All three Yankee batters struck out in the fifth, seventh and ninth innings.

The Yankees had 99 error-free games in 2007, a single-season team record. For the season, the Yankees committed just 88 errors. Only three players had more than five: Derek Jeter (18), Robinson Cano (13) and Alex Rodriguez (13).

David Cone pitched the third perfect game in Yankee history against the Montreal Expos on July 18, 1999, just one season after David Wells' perfect game. Don Larsen, who threw New York's first perfect game, threw out the ceremonial first pitch.

New York swept the Atlanta Braves in the 1999 World Series by winning Game 4 by a score of 4-1. Mariano Rivera was named MVP after recording one win and two saves.

By The Numbers

• • • ○○○

New York Yankees

B
A
S
E
B
A
L
L

The Yankees have lost 100 more games in a season twice. The club lost 102 games in 1912 and 103 games in 1908.

The Yankees have won 100 or more games in a season seven times and failed to win the World Series: 1942, 1954, 1963, 1980 and 2002-04.

New York has won 100 or more games in a season 19 times. The last time was in 2009 when the team finished the season with a 103-59 regular-season record.

Lou Gehrig had nine seasons with 200 or more hits (1927, 1928, 1930-34, 1936 and 1937), more than Babe Ruth and Joe DiMaggio combined. Ruth surpassed 200 hits three times (1921, 1923 and 1924) and DiMaggio accomplished the feat twice (1936 and 1937).

The last season the leading Yankee had less than 100 RBIs was in 1995. Paul O'Neil led the team with 96 RBIs. As a team, New York finished with 709 RBIs, the last time the Yankees finished with less than 750 RBIs.

New York recorded its 100th win on June 19, 1904, with a 4-3 victory against the St. Louis Browns.

The Yankees won 100 or more games during three consecutive seasons from 2002-04. This was a first for New York and the fifth time in Major League Baseball history.

By The Numbers

*All information in this book is valid
as of the end of the
2010 season.*